LONDON'S SOUTH BANK
IN 50 BUILDINGS

LOUIS BERK & RACHEL KOLSKY

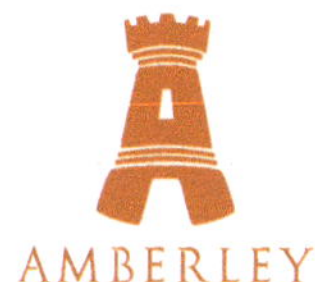

AMBERLEY

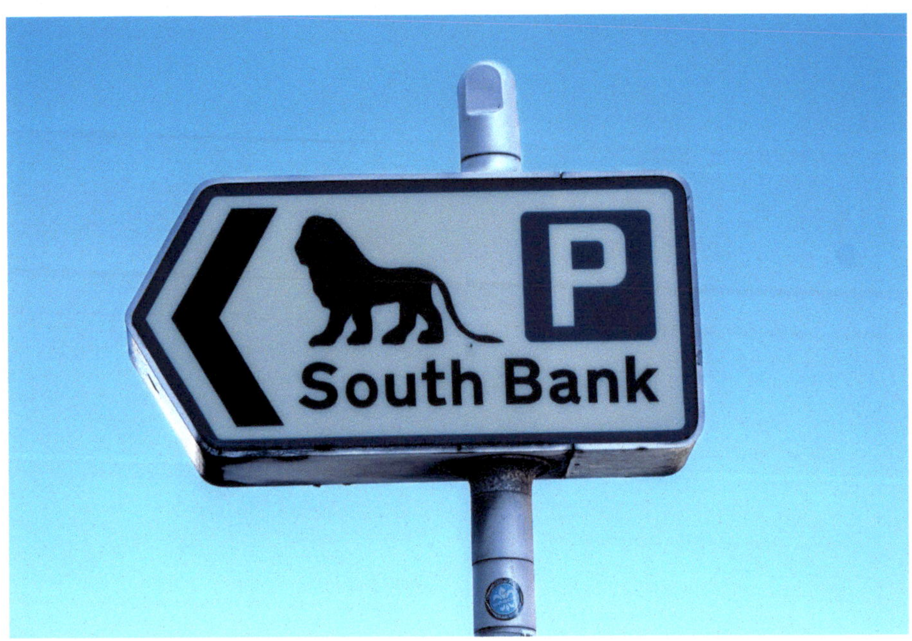
Iconic 1960s signpost near Waterloo Bridge.

First published 2024

Amberley Publishing, The Hill, Stroud
Gloucestershire GL5 4EP

www.amberley-books.com

Copyright © Louis Berk & Rachel Kolsky, 2024

The right of Louis Berk & Rachel Kolsky to be identified as the Authors of this work has been asserted in accordance with the Copyrights, Designs and Patents Act 1988.

Map contains Ordnance Survey data © Crown copyright and database right [2024]

British Library Cataloguing in Publication Data.
A catalogue record for this book is available from the British Library.

ISBN 978 1 3981 1003 8 (print)
ISBN 978 1 3981 1004 5 (ebook)

Typesetting by SJmagic DESIGN SERVICES, India.
Printed in Great Britain.

Contents

Map   4

Key   5

A Welcome from the Authors   7

The 50 Buildings   9

About the Authors and Acknowledgements   95

How to use this book

The buildings are listed as seen walking eastwards from Vauxhall bus station towards Tower Bridge. Where an entry is a listed building, this indicates it is designated a nationally important and protected building, graded by Historic England (historicengland.org.uk). The map enables you to locate the buildings within the book, as the key uses the same numbers as the text. Information regarding transport and websites was correct at the time of writing. Transport for London (tfl.gov.uk) is an excellent resource for planning journeys, and before visiting any of the buildings with public access it is advisable to check their individual websites for opening hours. The map is indicative only and not to scale. Each entry has the full address and postcode for ease of locating.

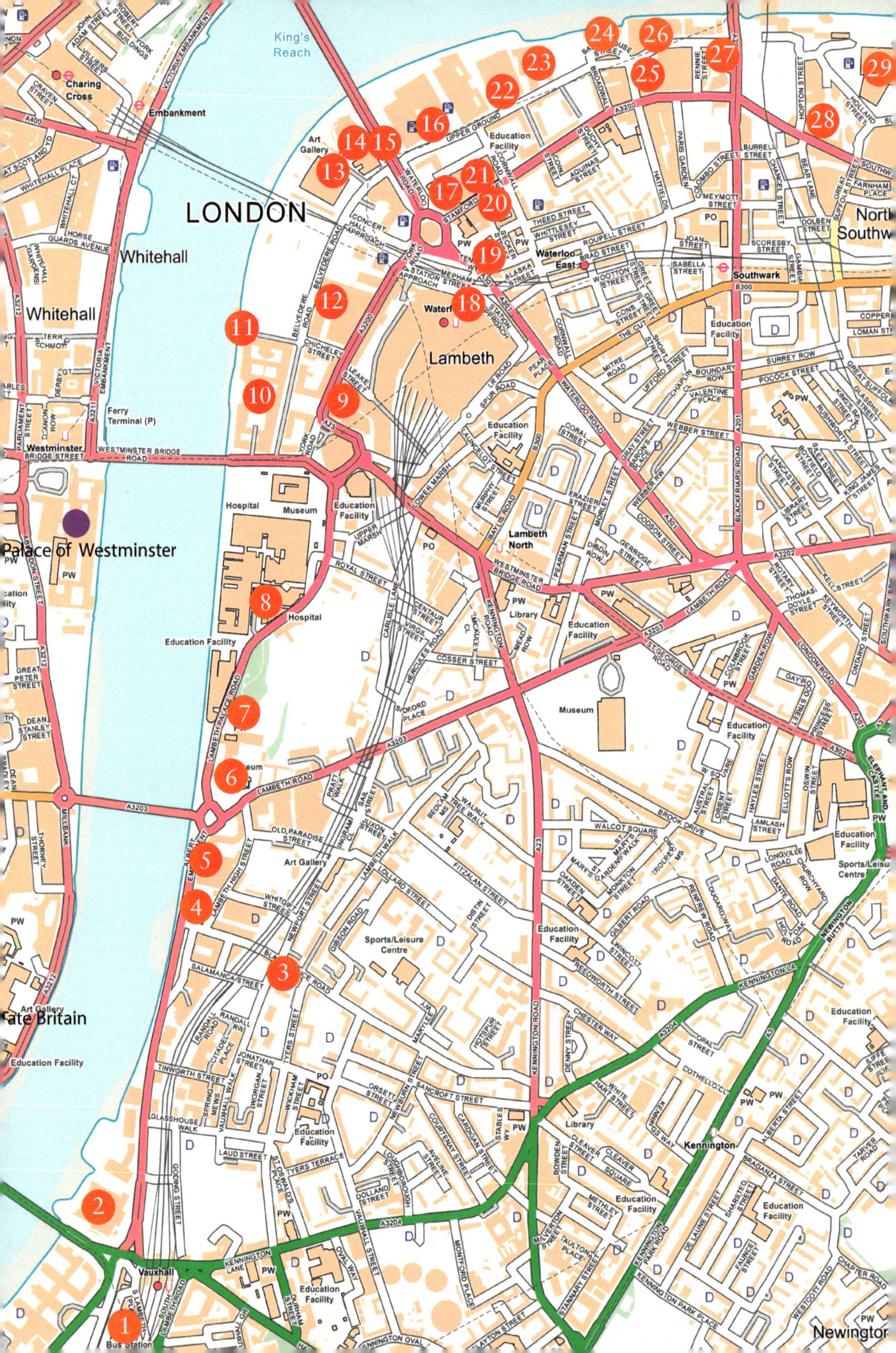

King's Reach
LONDON
Whitehall
Whitehall
Palace of Westminster
Tate Britain
Lambeth
North Southwark
Southwark
Charing Cross
Embankment
Waterloo East
Waterloo
Lambeth North
Westminster
Vauxhall
Kennington
Newington
Art Gallery
Education Facility
Hospital
Museum
Library
Sports/Leisure Centre
PO
PW

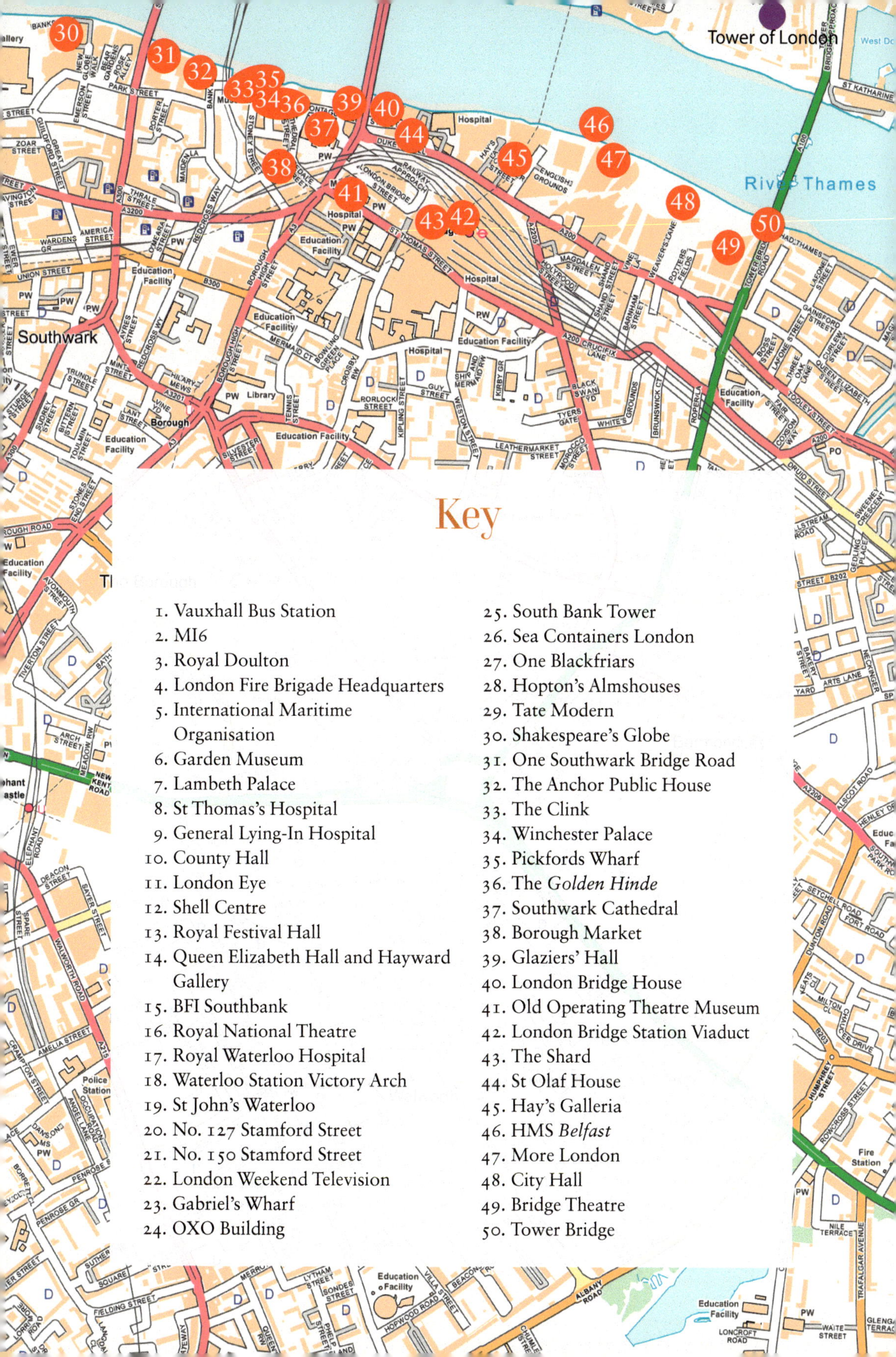

Key

1. Vauxhall Bus Station
2. MI6
3. Royal Doulton
4. London Fire Brigade Headquarters
5. International Maritime Organisation
6. Garden Museum
7. Lambeth Palace
8. St Thomas's Hospital
9. General Lying-In Hospital
10. County Hall
11. London Eye
12. Shell Centre
13. Royal Festival Hall
14. Queen Elizabeth Hall and Hayward Gallery
15. BFI Southbank
16. Royal National Theatre
17. Royal Waterloo Hospital
18. Waterloo Station Victory Arch
19. St John's Waterloo
20. No. 127 Stamford Street
21. No. 150 Stamford Street
22. London Weekend Television
23. Gabriel's Wharf
24. OXO Building
25. South Bank Tower
26. Sea Containers London
27. One Blackfriars
28. Hopton's Almshouses
29. Tate Modern
30. Shakespeare's Globe
31. One Southwark Bridge Road
32. The Anchor Public House
33. The Clink
34. Winchester Palace
35. Pickfords Wharf
36. The *Golden Hinde*
37. Southwark Cathedral
38. Borough Market
39. Glaziers' Hall
40. London Bridge House
41. Old Operating Theatre Museum
42. London Bridge Station Viaduct
43. The Shard
44. St Olaf House
45. Hay's Galleria
46. HMS *Belfast*
47. More London
48. City Hall
49. Bridge Theatre
50. Tower Bridge

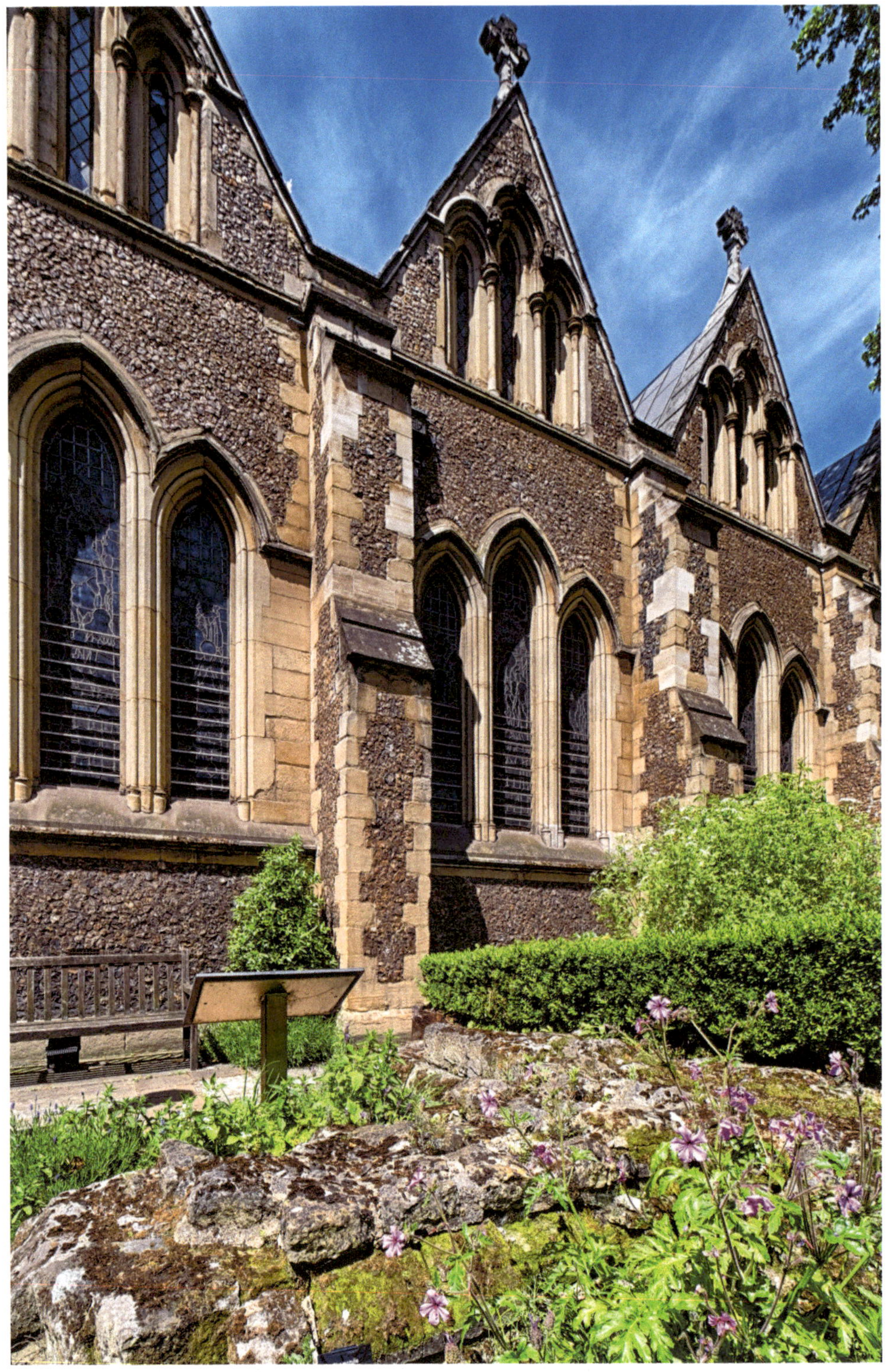

The medieval herb garden at Southwark Cathedral (see entry 37).

A Welcome from the Authors

The River Thames flowing through London is often taken for granted but more than anything else in the city it has been witness to the rise, demise and renaissance of London as a trading and residential metropolis. The north bank, site of Roman Londinium, grew westwards, associated with pomp and ceremony, government and monarchy and of course finance in the Square Mile, and so it remains today. The south bank was home to fun and recreation, trade and commerce. Centuries ago London banned theatres and pleasure gardens, necessitating such venues to be sited across the river at Bankside where bear baiting, cockfighting and several theatres could be found. Wharves, warehouses and light industry lined the riverside both east and west of Tower Bridge. Following substantial Second World War bomb damage and closure of the docks in the late 1960s, the riverside and immediate hinterland suffered a rapid decline.

A respite in 1951 with the Festival of Britain was brief with the regeneration of the southern waterside only beginning in earnest some decades later. The transformation has been astonishing and *London's South Bank in 50 Buildings* will take you on a journey from Vauxhall Bridge to Tower Bridge, walking through riverside Lambeth and Southwark, passing fourteen road, pedestrian and railway bridges and discovering an array of buildings with significant histories through which you discover the development of London from the Middle Ages through to the present day. For many, the south bank is the entertainment area between Westminster and Waterloo bridges but our south bank takes you further west and east. Many buildings, such as Shakespeare's Globe and The Shard, are recognised globally but we also profile lesser-known buildings that have fascinating but little-known histories. Indeed, it was not until the late 1960s that plans took shape to open up riverside walkways to the public, with the Queen Elizabeth's Silver Jubilee walkway in 1977 literally paving the way.

The route is now one of the most delightful in London including old neighbourhoods with new personalities. Not only the Southbank Centre (SBC) but Jubilee Gardens alongside County Hall and the London Eye, Bankside centred on the decommissioned power station, and More London, an area once dominated by river trade and railway traffic, now a lively working, living and entertainment district. In between there are buildings linked to maternity care, garden history, spies, worship, medicine, ceramics, incarceration, warfare and social housing. There are David vs Goliath battles between residents and developers and a glorious array of architectural details to discover.

Although the book profiles only buildings on the south bank, you will discover that from the south bank there are spectacular views of the north bank, including the Palace of Westminster, St Paul's Cathedral and the City's dense cluster of steel and glass. Many of these building appear in our companion book *London's North Bank in 50 Buildings*.

As with our other Amberley books, *Whitechapel in 50 Buildings* and *Secret Whitechapel*, *London's South Bank in 50 Buildings* can be used both as a guidebook and as a reference to the area's rich and varied history. Although the book begins at Vauxhall, you can reverse your walking route starting at Tower Bridge and you can do it all in one go, or in stages, planning time in the museums, galleries and other points of interest outlined en route. Enjoy!

Louis Berk and Rachel Kolsky
Summer 2023

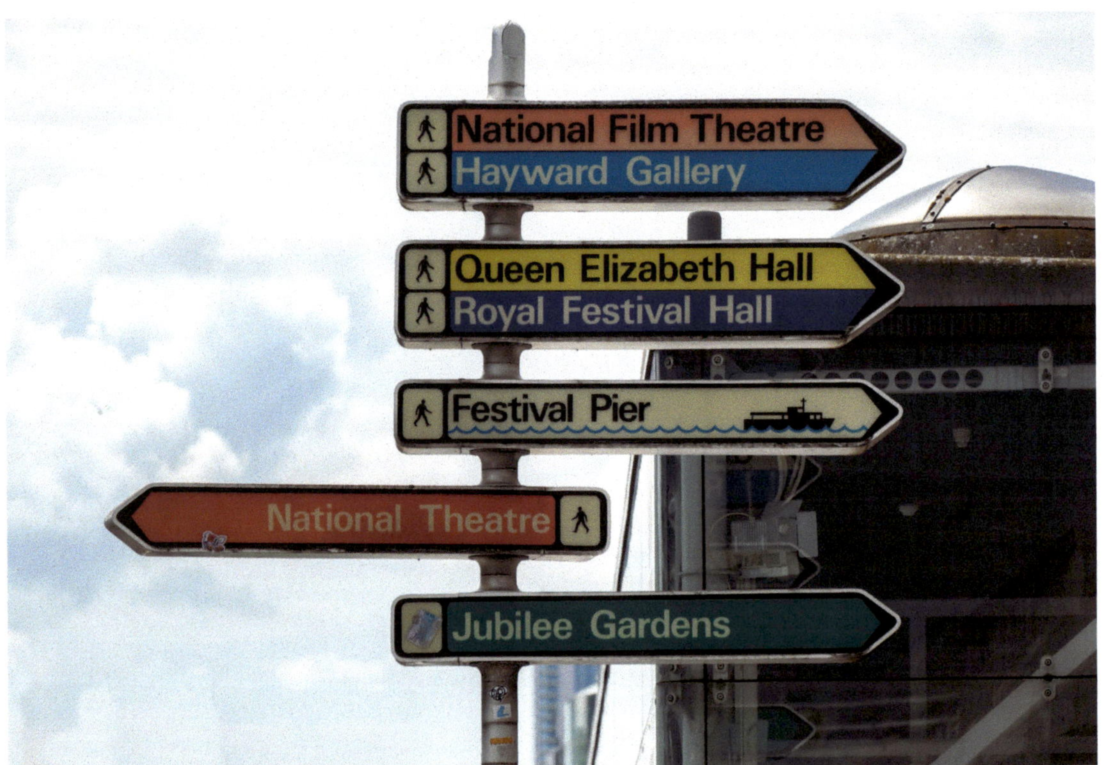

Distinctive signage at the Southbank Centre.

The 50 Buildings

1. Vauxhall Bus Station

Each day Vauxhall Cross traffic junction sees thousands of cars and buses driving by, while the tube and mainline stations together receive over 1,400 trains. By the early 2000s this complex interchange required substantial streamlining and the junction's facelift incorporated a new bus garage.

Resembling a ski-jump and designed by Arup Associates, it opened in 2005 as a striking, unmissable landmark for a previously challenging road intersection. Vauxhall's stainless steel structure, 200 metres long, 12 metres wide and set at a jaunty angle of 20 degrees, was light, shiny and glamorous. Lighting was generated through rooftop photovoltaic cells and the undulating roof line allowed for double decker buses to manoeuvre easily. However, the bus station remained surrounded by traffic and by 2011 plans by Marks Barfield, London Eye architects (see Entry 11), suggested a skywalk instead. This scheme was shelved but in 2019 plans were approved to return to a two-way

An iconic red New Routemaster bus exits the Vauxhall bus garage.

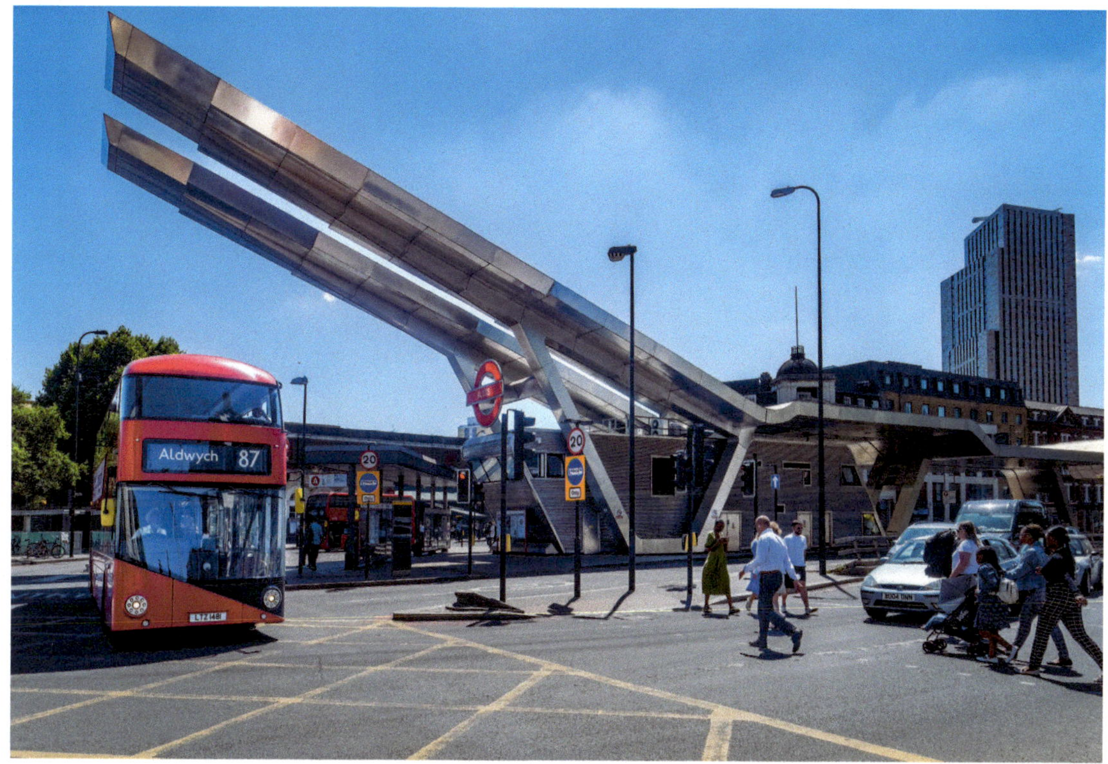

road system, necessitating demolition, making way for two tower blocks incorporating a hotel, commercial units, retail outlets, residences, a pedestrian square and a new smaller bus station. However, currently the bus station survives.

Address: Vauxhall Cross, SW8 1SJ
Built: 2005 – Arup Associates
Public Access: Yes
Tube/Rail: Vauxhall

2. MI6

To the east of Vauxhall Bridge is the headquarters of the UK's Secret Intelligence Service, better known as MI6. MI stands for Military Intelligence, with MI5 responsible for domestic security and MI6 for international surveillance. Built between 1990 and 1994 and opened by Queen Elizabeth II, architect Terry Farrell's inimitable design in postmodernist style, a short-lived architectural form characterised by playful designs often featuring coloured building materials and rounded skylines, was one of three high-profile projects he

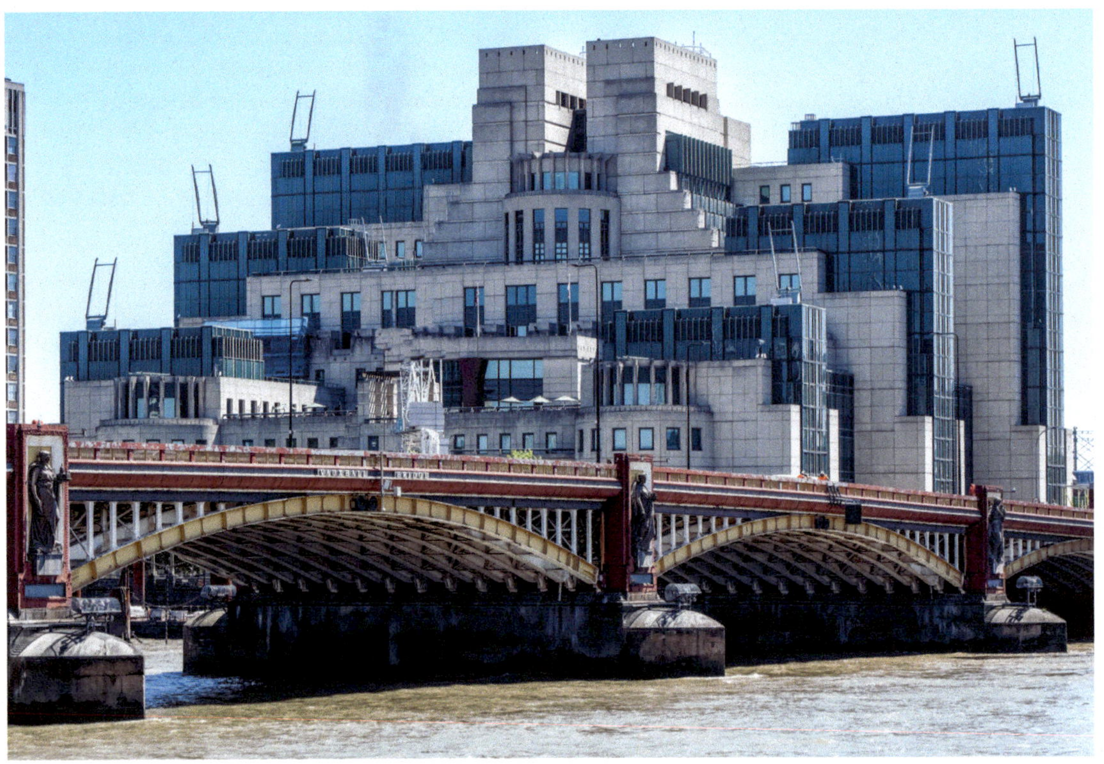

MI6 Headquarters and Vauxhall Bridge.

completed within a few years (the others being Embankment Place above Charing Cross station and TV-am at Camden Town) and produced mixed reviews.

MI6 was apparently inspired by the art deco Battersea Power Station not far away but architectural critics see the design as influenced by the Aztecs or Mayans of central America. The light-hearted exterior belies the cost of the construction. It had to include an estimated forty to sixty roofs, bomb-resistant stonework and triple-glazed windows. The dark green glazing is opaque but light can stream in through the vertical 'fins'.

The exterior has featured in two James Bond films, *The World Is Not Enough* in 1999 and *Spectre* in 2015, while the interior has been used in five other Bond films.

Address: No. 85 Albert Embankment, SE1 7TP
Built: 1990/94 – Terry Farrell
Public Access: No
Tube/Rail: Vauxhall

3. Royal Doulton

A peek down Black Prince Road brings into view a wonderfully exuberant corner building. Built in 1871 (with later extensions) as Royal Doulton's design studio, art school and ceramic museum, the exterior also acted as an open-air salesroom displaying the different styles of glazed pottery which Doulton was already famous for. The business closed in 1956 and most of the premises were demolished. Some friezes were saved and are now in the Victoria & Albert Museum. The name Doulton survives high up on the original façade. The building is five storeys high, with windows providing additional visual impact in square, pointed, circular and Tudor styles. At ground floor level is an array of glossy ceramics illustrating colours available for glazing together with sample designs including flower motifs, curvaceous blue leaves and ears of wheat.

John Doulton first established his pottery in Fulham, moving to Vauxhall Walk in 1815 and Lambeth Walk in 1826. In 1846, Doulton's son Henry moved the business to the Albert Embankment, producing up to 13 miles per week of glazed piping, meeting the growing demand for better public health and sanitation. Additional factories in Dudley and St Helens manufactured piping for the Post Office and a rapidly growing railway network. When their partner Watts retired in 1854 the name changed to Doulton & Co. and from the 1860s their range expanded to over seventy products. Doulton employed students from the nearby Lambeth School of Art including over 100 women. Above the Lambeth High Street corner entrance an 1878 terracotta relief depicts people perusing vases, a lady making a pot and a cat below her chair. In 1901 King Edward VII granted a royal warrant and the name became Royal Doulton. By the 1950s the company's salt-glaze methods did not comply with London's new clean air regulations and Royal Doulton transferred production to Stoke.

Subsequently used by the DVLA and as a London Black Cab driver test centre, it is now Southbank House, offering shared workspace units and art studios.

Alongside the Embankment is White Hart Dock. Dating back to the 1300s and due to be closed off from the river in the 1960s, it became disused but in 2009 was imaginatively renovated with decorative wooden arches above the surviving dock and *Standing Boats*, a group of wooden benches shaped as river vessels.

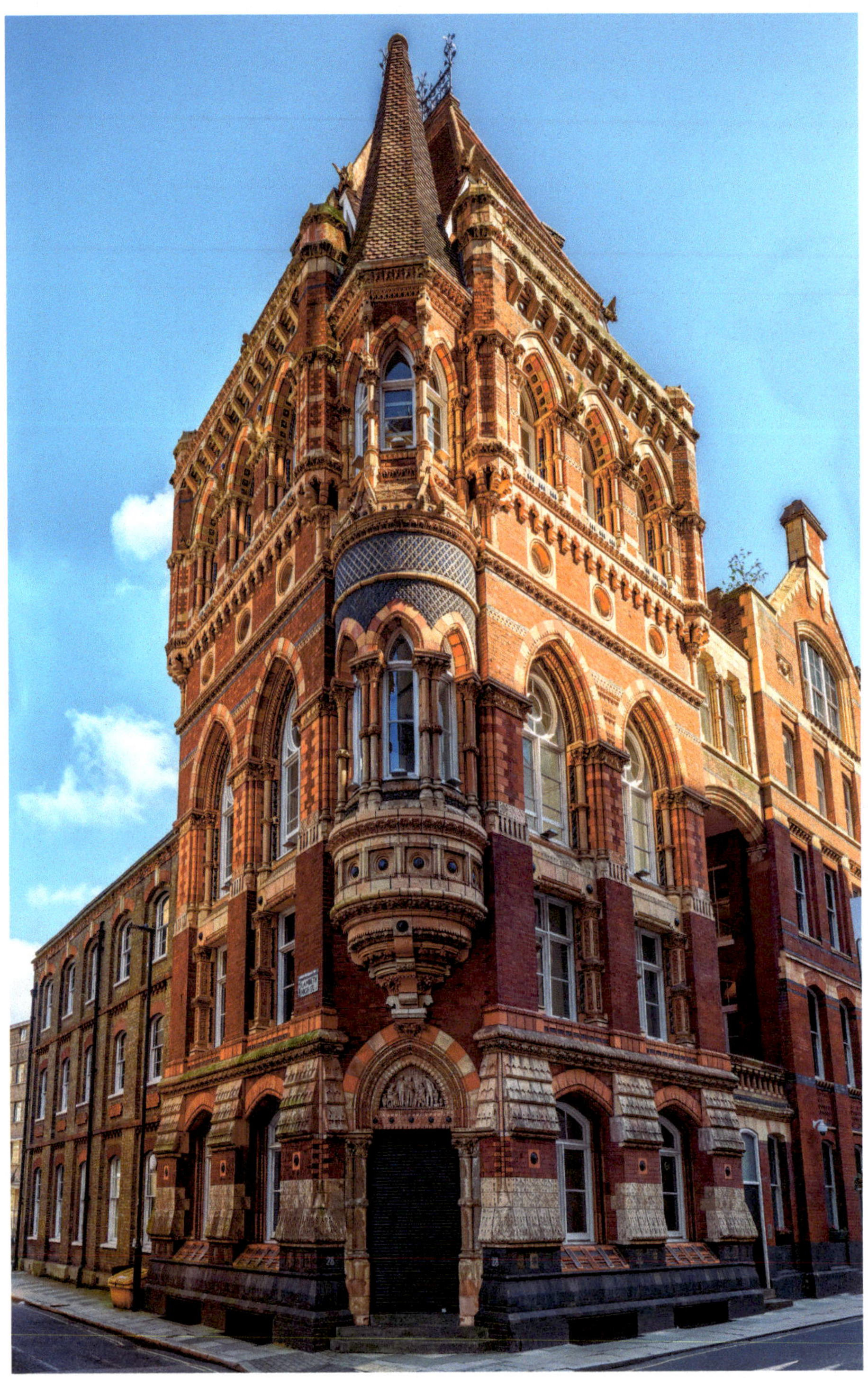

Royal Doulton Factory.

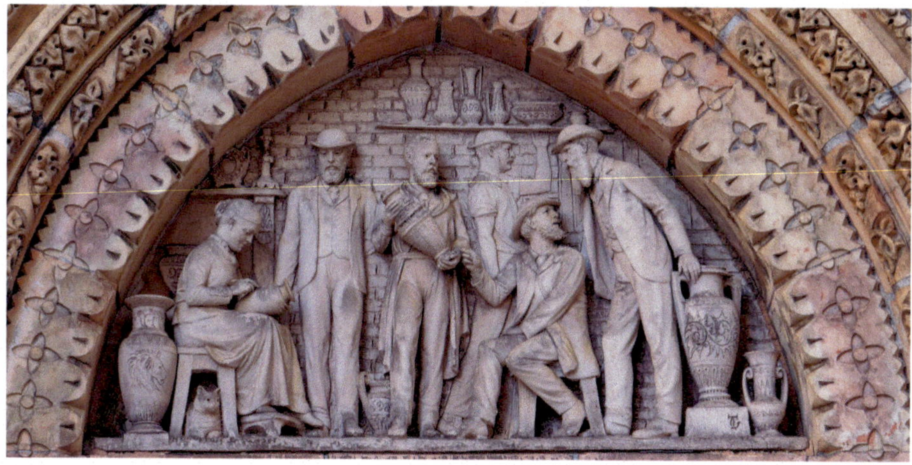

Above: Frieze over the entrance to the Doulton Factory.

Below left: Examples of Doulton ware decorate the factory exterior.

Below right: White Hart Dock with distinctive boat-shaped benches.

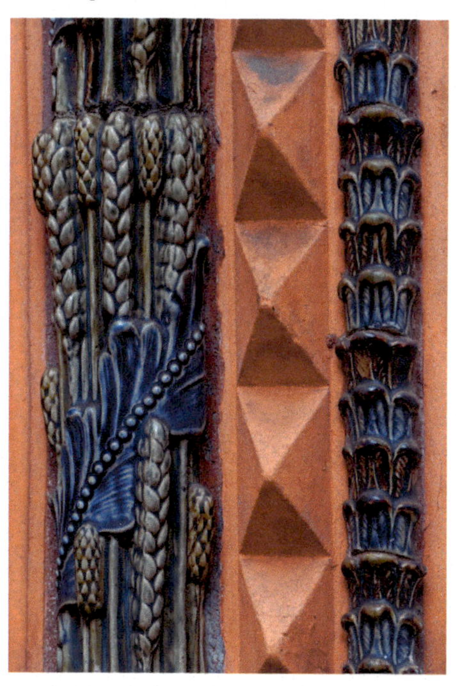

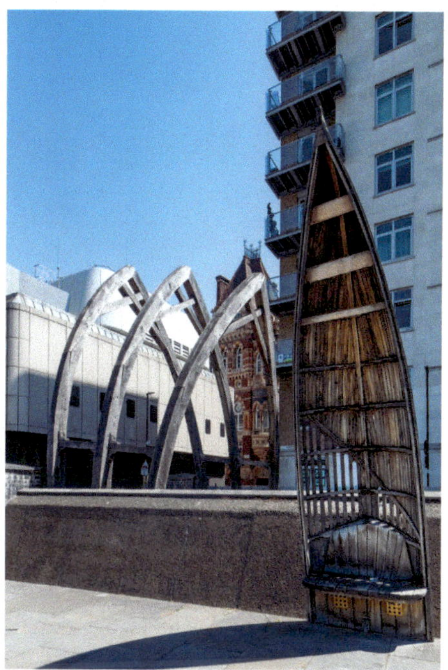

Address: Black Prince Road, SE1 7SJ
Built: 1876/78
Listed Status: Grade II
Public Access: No
Tube/Rail: Lambeth North, Waterloo

4. London Fire Brigade Headquarters

At the corner of Black Prince Road and Albert Embankment – reclaimed as part of the Joseph Balzalgette sewerage project following the Great Stink of 1858 – stands the second headquarters of the London Fire Brigade (LFB). Built on land once owned by Doulton (see Entry 3) and opened by King George VI and Queen Elizabeth in 1937, the building is a fine example of moderne architecture. The steel-framed structure is clad in brown-grey brick and the ground floor houses seven vehicle bays, with three storeys for administrative offices and four for accommodation. The rear of the building, designed for fire demonstrations, has a stepped grandstand arrangement with capacity for 800 people.

Below ground is a separate bomb- and gas-proof structure, completed in time for the Second World War when the building became central to the LFB's response to the Blitz.

Reflecting its importance, several sculptures were commissioned for the Albert Embankment façade. Either side of the vehicle bays are panelled doors with friezes by Nicholas Babb depicting firemen in action. In the centre from the third floor upwards, classical friezes by Gilbert Bayes portray mermen with hoses, Phoebus in his chariot and ears of wheat. Topping out the decoration is the distinctive London County Council crest carved in stone. Other unmistakeably moderne architectural details include panelled doors, decorative grilles, distinctive steel windows and Portland stone cornices.

Former London Fire Brigade Headquarters.

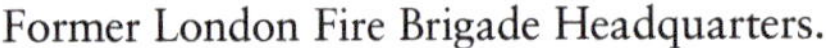

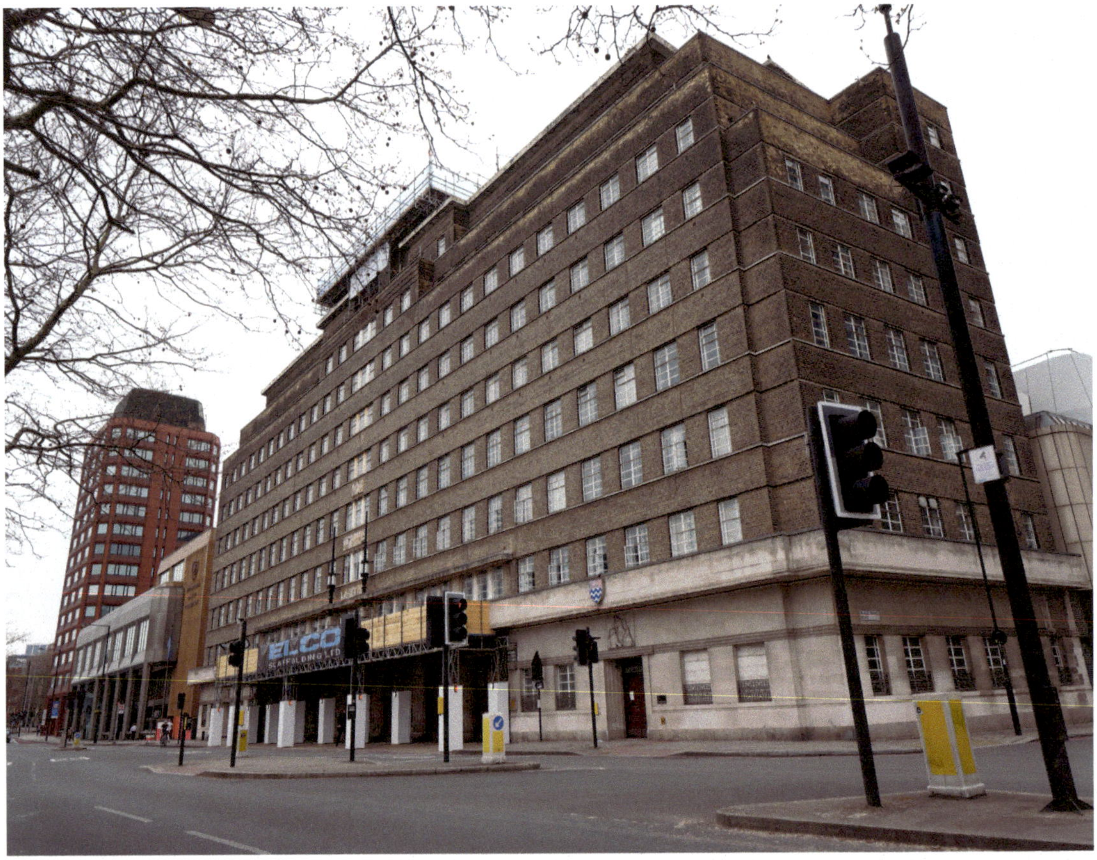

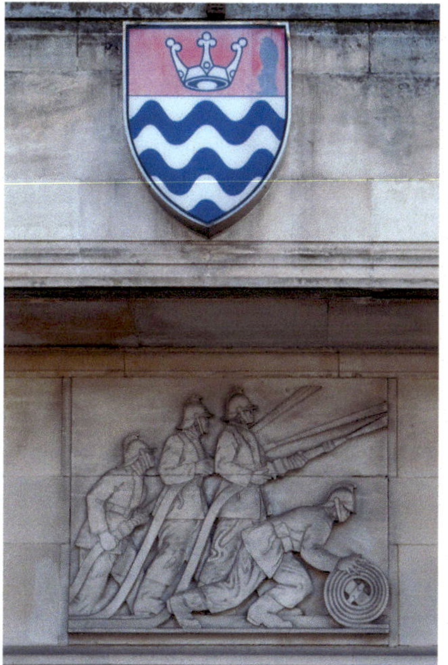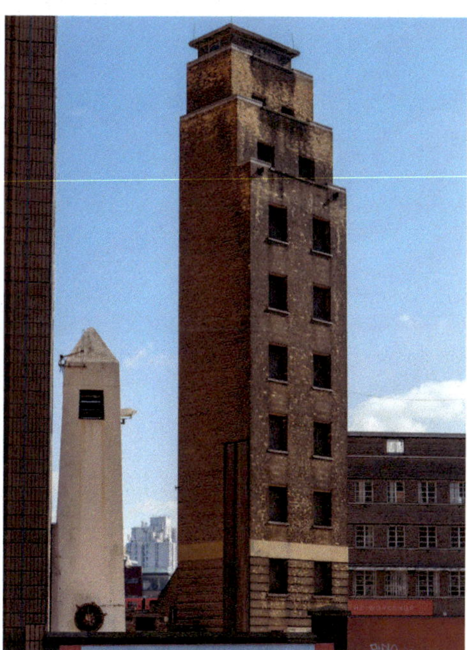

Above left: Relief of firemen in action.

Above right: Nine-storey drill tower.

The building ceased as LFB headquarters in 2008 but remains a fire station with accommodation. Current plans to redevelop the immediate neighbourhood include a museum celebrating the LFB's history and heritage.

Address: No. 8 Albert Embankment, SE1 7SD
Built: 1937 – EP Wheeler
Listed Status: Grade II (Building, Drill Tower)
Public Access: No
Tube: Vauxhall

5. International Maritime Organisation

Opened in 1983 by Queen Elizabeth II, the International Maritime Organisation (IMO) building was commissioned as offices for 300 international civil servants including a conference hall, meeting spaces and a fourth-floor roof terrace. Specially commissioned works of art throughout the building represent oceans and maritime trade and at ground level are models of ships and vessels linked to merchant shipping, which still accounts for 90 per cent of international trade.

Established in 1948 by the United Nations (UN) as the Inter Governmental Maritime Consultative Organisation, it eliminated confusion caused by each country having developed its own regulations for ports, fees and paperwork.

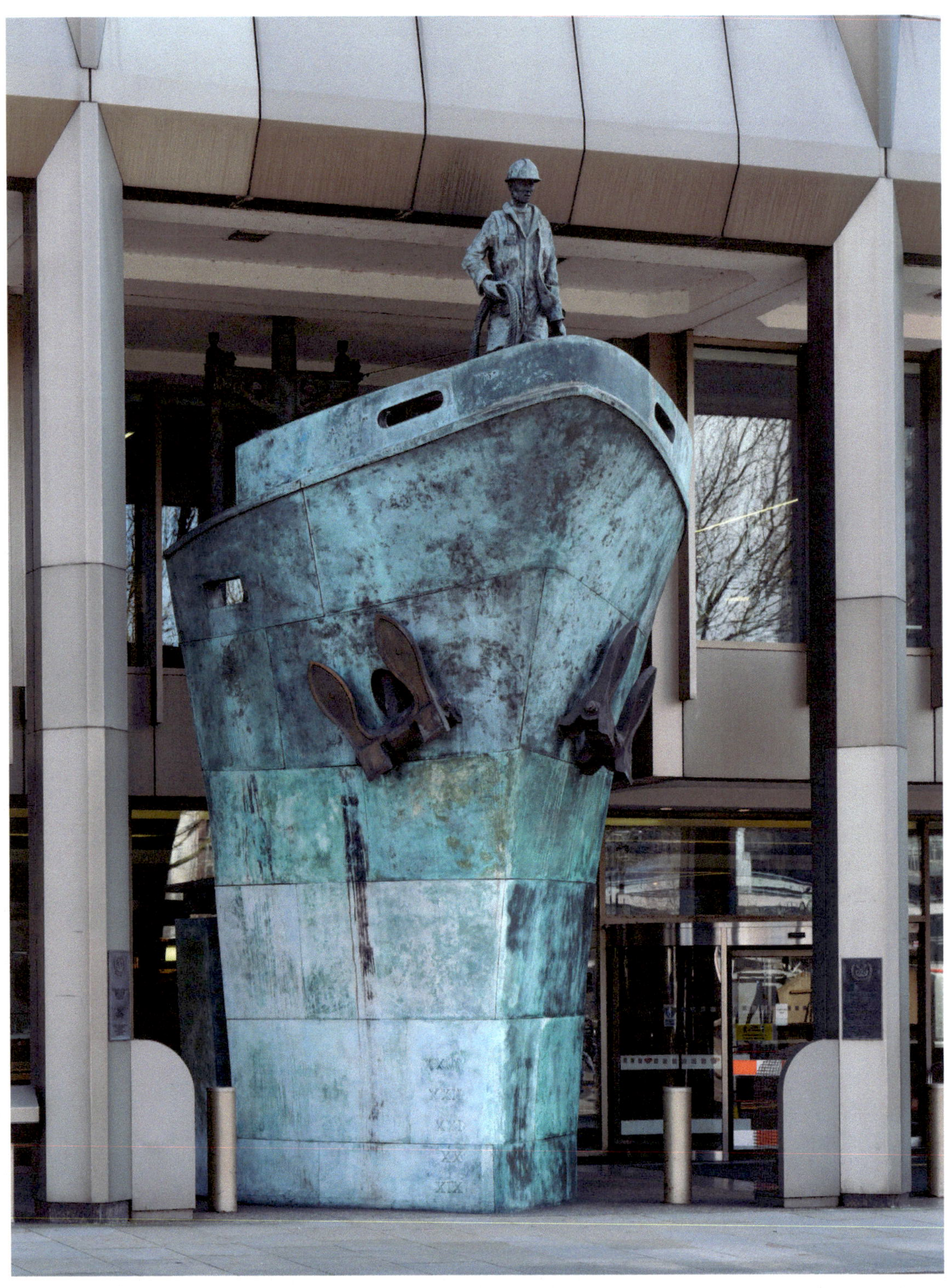

Seafarers' Memorial, International Maritime Organisation.

The IMO's key responsibilities are safety and security at sea, including piracy, safety codes, pollution and, from 1988, global search and rescue. The IMO is also responsible for interaction between ships and ports, training and legal matters pertaining to sea trade. It is the only UN agency headquartered in the UK.

The *International Memorial to Seafarers*, unveiled in 2001, provides a dramatic addition to the streetscape. Weighing 10 tons and standing 7 metres tall, the ship's brow and lone sailor symbolise the merchant seaman's sense of isolation where vast ships often have only a handful of crew. Designed by Michael Sandle, the classic cargo ship and anchor are reminders of shipping before the age of containers.

Address: No. 4 Albert Embankment, SE1 7SR
Built: 1977/82 – Douglas Marriott Worby & Robinson
Public Access: No
Tube/Rail: Lambeth North, Vauxhall
Website: imo.org

6. Garden Museum

St Mary's Church, originally a wooden structure founded in 1062, is today eclipsed as the oldest building in Lambeth only by the crypt of Lambeth Palace (see Entry 7). The tower is the only early remnant following rebuilding in 1852 but the crypt contains remains of many early Archbishops of Canterbury. By 1972 falling attendances and the need for extensive repairs led to

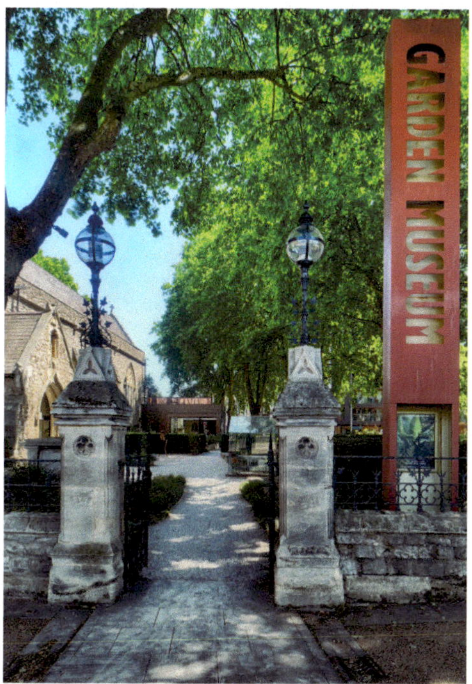

Garden Museum entrance.

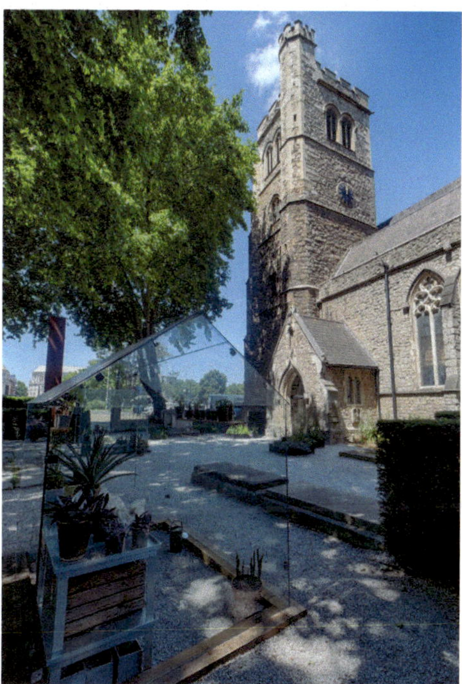

St Mary's Church tower.

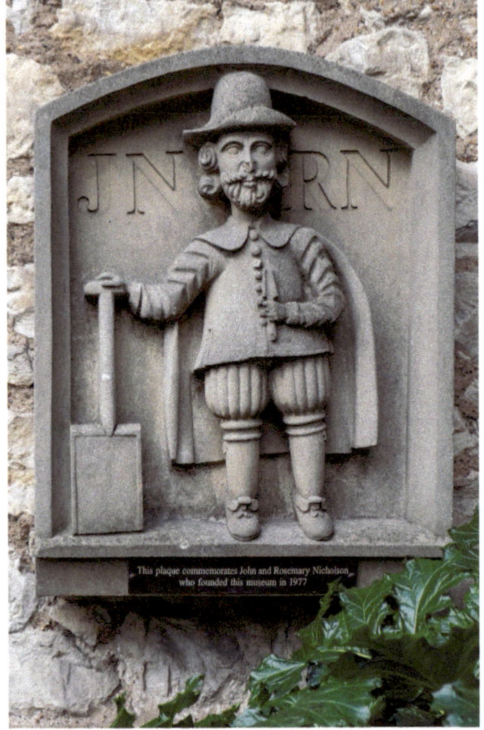

Plaque to the founders.

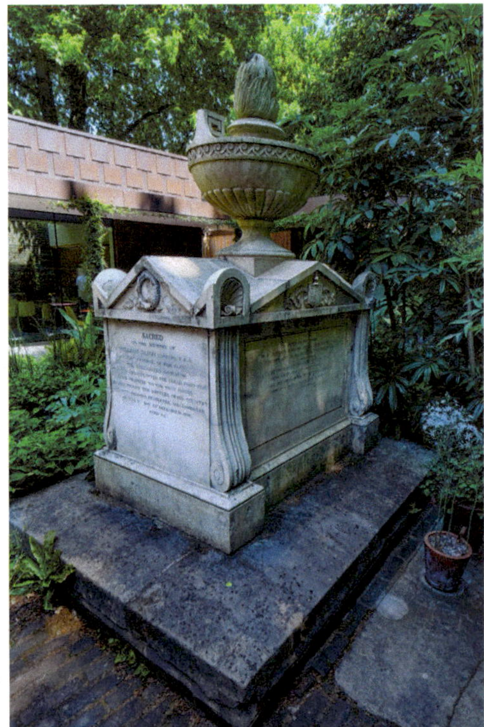

Tomb of William Bligh.

its decommissioning and scheduled demolition. It was saved by Rosemary and John Nicholson, who intervened preserving significant graves, including that of John Tradescant and his son, sixteenth/seventeenth-century seed and plant collectors who are credited with introducing England to species including the tulip and cultivating the first pineapple on English soil.

The Nicholsons established the Tradescant Trust, which purchased the building and converted it into the Garden Museum. Refurbished in the mid-2010s, it explores and celebrates British gardens and gardening through its collection and temporary exhibitions. Visitors can ascend the 131 steps of the church tower for panoramic views while the Sackler Garden to the rear with access to the church graveyard is a homage to the Tradescants.

Burials of former residents of Lambeth include Vice-Admiral William Bligh, a navigator and a colleague of Nelson but chiefly remembered for captaining the scientific expedition to acquire samples of the Tahitian breadfruit plant, during which his crew mutinied in 1789. Atop his tomb is a sculpture of an eternal flame, although some believe it represents the breadfruit.

Address: Lambeth Palace Road, SE1 7LB
Built: 1062, 1337, 1851/52; Garden Museum, 2015/17 – Dow Jones
Listed Status: Grade II*
Public Access: Yes
Tube: Lambeth North, Vauxhall, Waterloo
Website: gardenmuseum.org.uk

7. Lambeth Palace

The official London residence for the Archbishop of Canterbury is identified by a red brick gatehouse next to the Garden Museum (see Entry 6). Known as Morton's Tower, it was built in 1490 by Cardinal Morton, archbishop from 1486 until his death in 1500.

The Archbishop of Canterbury is the Church of England's most senior position and associations with Lambeth date back to 1190 when the Convent of St Andrew of Rochester sold part of its manor to Archbishop Baldwin. He acquired the rest of the manor in 1197, building a house on the south bank of the Thames opposite the Palace of Westminster. The first Archbishop of Canterbury to live here was Stephen Langton. The palace's eventful history includes the ransacking and subsequent murder of Archbishop Simon Sudbury during the 1381 Peasants' Revolt, the imprisonment of key clerics including Sir Thomas More and being repurposed as a prison during the seventeenth-century republic. The 1820s and 1830s witnessed major rebuilding works overseen by architect Edward Blore but only Morton's Tower remains visible to passersby.

From the 1200s until 1842 the poor of Lambeth would gather at the tower three times a week to receive the 'Lambeth Dole', charity given in the form of bread, broth and small money grants. The ground floor houses a cell dating from the 1500s. Extensive gardens lie behind the high brick walls but the estate was originally larger. From the late 1880s archbishops allowed local impoverished children to use part of the gardens as a playground, and in 1901 Archbishop Temple designated 20 acres as a public park. Named Archbishop's Park, one of the entrances is opposite St Thomas's Hospital (see Entry 8).

Morton's Tower, Lambeth Palace.

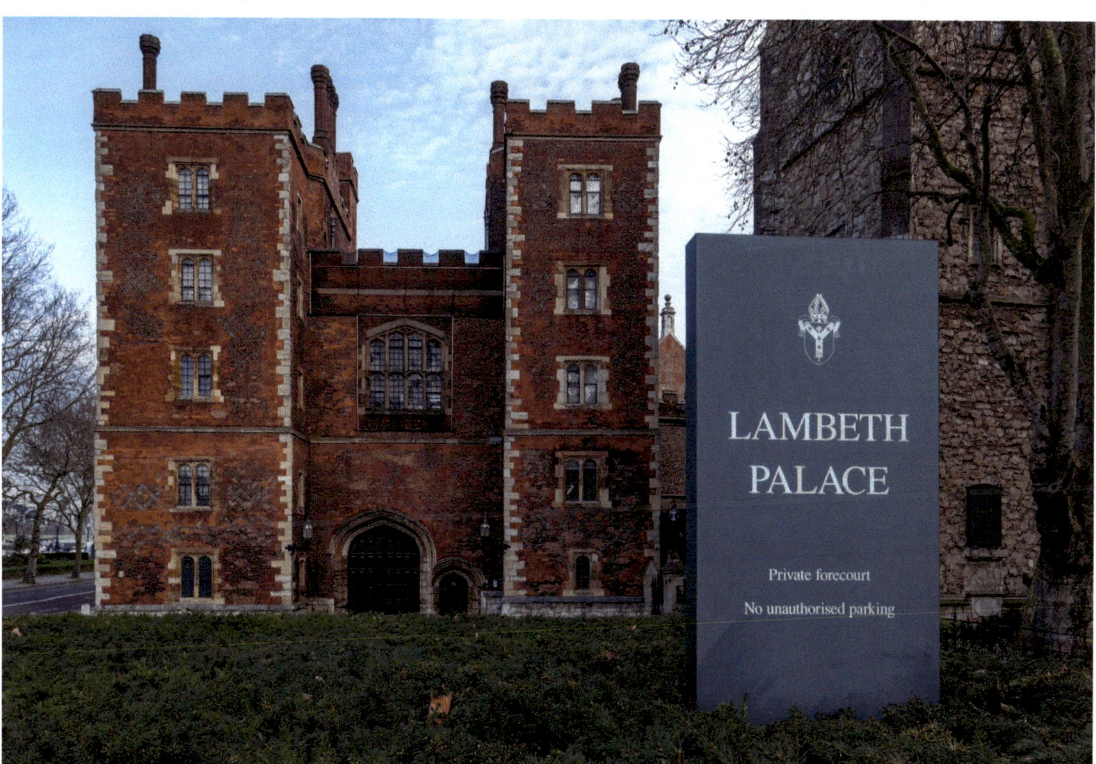

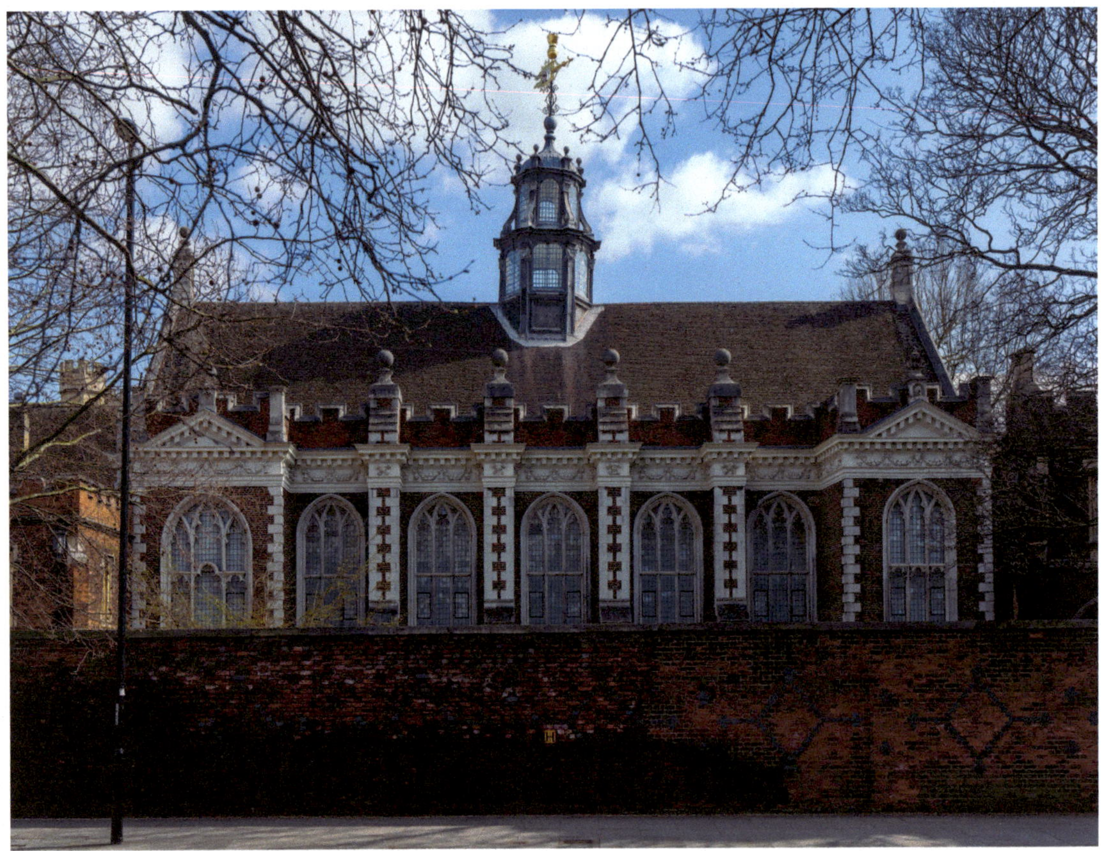

Lambeth Palace library.

At the time of writing, Archbishop Justin Welby is the 105th Archbishop of Canterbury.

Address: Lambeth Palace Road, SE1 7JU
Built: Various dating from 1485; extensive remodelling in the 1820s and 1830s
Listed Status: Grade I
Public Access: Intermittent. Check website for details
Tube/Rail: Lambeth North, Waterloo, Westminster
Website: archbishopofcanterbury.org

8. St Thomas's Hospital

St Thomas's Hospital's Italianate 274-metre frontage provides a striking contrast to the Victorian Gothic Palace of Westminster opposite.

Dating back to 1106, the hospital's original site (see Entry 41) was acquired for London Bridge station (see Entry 42) in 1859, opening here in 1871 with six blocks constructed according to the theories of Florence Nightingale, the nurse who famously transformed the Scutari military hospital during the 1854/56 Crimean War and pioneered nurse training. She promoted the importance of ventilation, natural light,

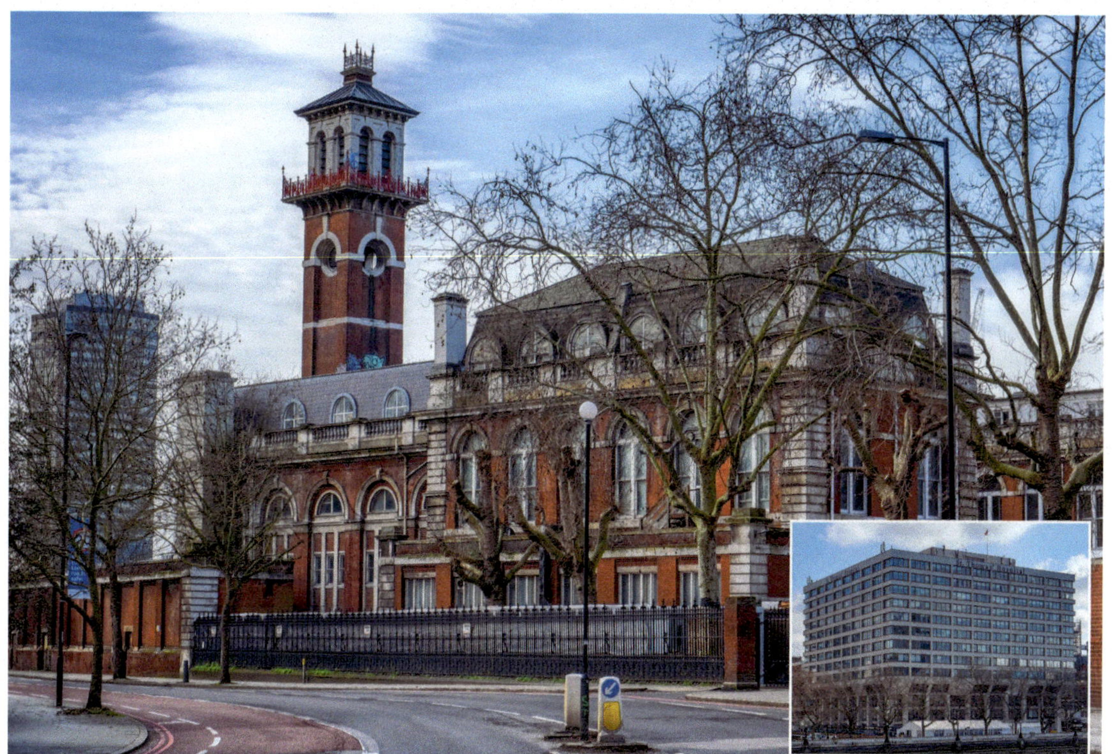

Water tower, St Thomas's Hospital. *Insert*: 1960s/70s hospital block overlooking the Thames.

fire prevention and the segregation of different facilities such as laundry, catering and sanitation from the wards.

When Florence's Training School of Nursing reopened here in 1900, there were eleven specialised outpatient departments in addition to in-patient care. The style is based on the miasmatic principle, prevalent at the time, that disease was airborne (rather than germ based) with long, narrow but not particularly high buildings with tall windows. A separate north block housed the administrative offices, governors' hall and committee room with the medical school to the south.

Additions were made in the early, mid- and late twentieth century but following war damage just three of the seven nineteenth-century pavilions survive. Plans are underway to transform Block 9, the original Medical School, and the 1978 Prideaux Building, providing additional workspaces and increased public access.

The eastern side of St Thomas's Hospital was rebuilt during the 1960/70s, with several public sculptures including one of Mary Seacole, another Crimea nurse, installed in the pedestrian plaza.

Address: Westminster Bridge Road, SE1 7EH
Built: 1868/71 – Henry Currey; additions 1901, 1904, 1925; 1966/75 – Yorke Rosenberg Mardall
Listed Status: South Wing – Grade II, Block 9, Medical School – Grade II
Public Access: Yes
Tube/Rail: Waterloo, Westminster
Website: guysandstthomas.nhs.uk

9. General Lying In Hospital

Amid the grey expanse of York Road sits an incongruous late eighteenth-century classical building with a grand entrance behind four Ionic columns: the Westminster New Lying-In Hospital. Opened in 1767 as a maternity hospital for married women, its name changed to General in 1818, relocating to York Road in 1828. By then the hospital was open to all Londoners, including unmarried women. A royal charter was granted in 1830 and modernisation and expansion continued throughout the nineteenth century, with a nurses' home added in 1907.

In 1933 Queen Mary opened a new wing with an outpatients department, additional nurses' accommodation and welfare centre. Following the Second World War it became the maternity wing for St Thomas's Hospital (see Entry 8) but closed in 1971, being repurposed in 2003 for NHS training, IT and procurement. It was sold in 2007; the 1930s nurses' home was demolished and a Premier Inn built alongside incorporating the hospital. The staircase leading to the original doorway remains unrenovated, contrasting with the grand newer lettering above. Behind the hospital is Leake Street, famous as a graffiti tunnel but the name commemorates Dr John Leake, the hospital's founder.

Address: No. 85 York Road, SE1 7NJ
Built: 1828
Listed Status: Grade II
Public Access: No
Tube/Rail: Waterloo
Website: premierinn.com

General Lying-in Hospital.

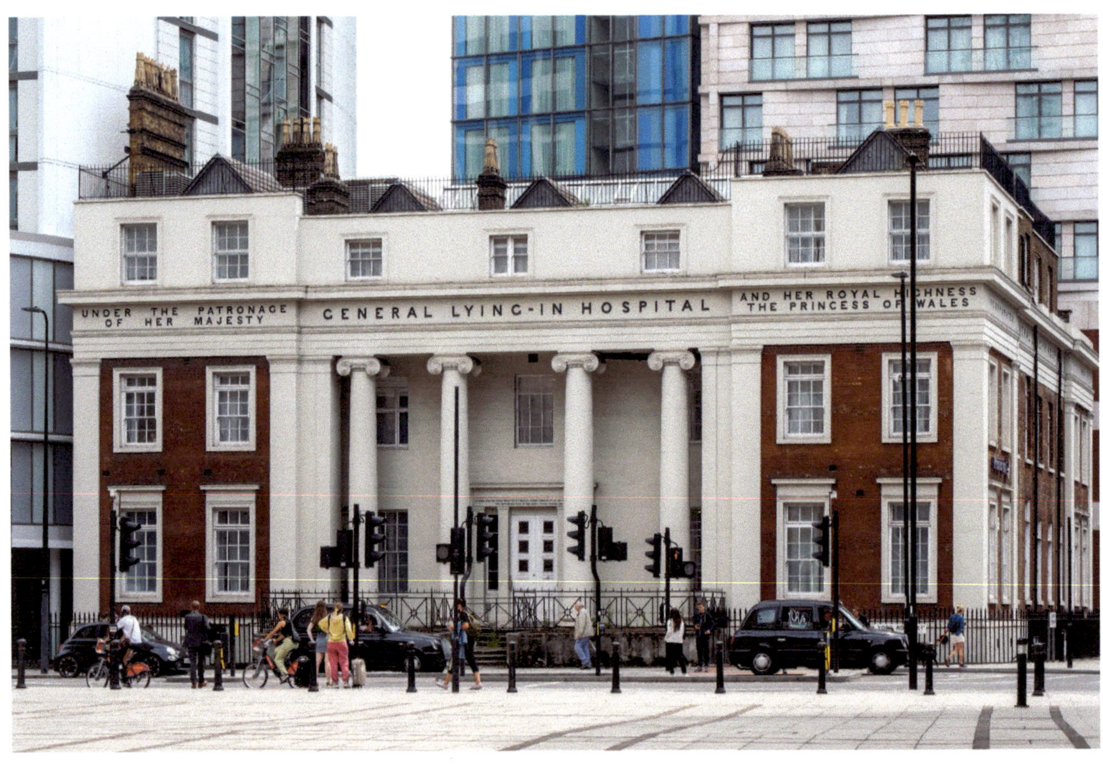

10. County Hall

Since the opening of the London Eye (see Entry 11) the riverside frontage of County Hall has become one of London's most recognisable sites.

It was commissioned as the headquarters for the London County Council (LCC), which in 1888 had replaced the Metropolitan Board of Works as the London-wide organisation responsible for public services. By 1911 the LCC had outgrown its Trafalgar Square premises, London's population having grown to 4.5 million, and construction on the new building began. Delayed by two world wars, it was finally completed in 1958.

The vast six-storey building of Portland stone on a Cornish granite plinth was designed by Ralph Knott in Edwardian baroque style and the first stages were opened in 1922 by King George V. Later blocks, in a neo-Edwardian baroque style to the north and south, date from the mid-1930s, making a complex of seven buildings. In 1974 the island block further south was completed.

The offices were the hub of London's administration until 1986 when the Greater London Council, which replaced the LCC in 1965, was controversially abolished. County Hall became empty, forlorn and unloved until acquired by a Japanese property investor. The 1970s southern annex was later demolished for the Park Plaza hotel and the north block remodelled to incorporate a ticket office for the London Eye and other visitor attractions, serviced apartments and eateries.

County Hall.

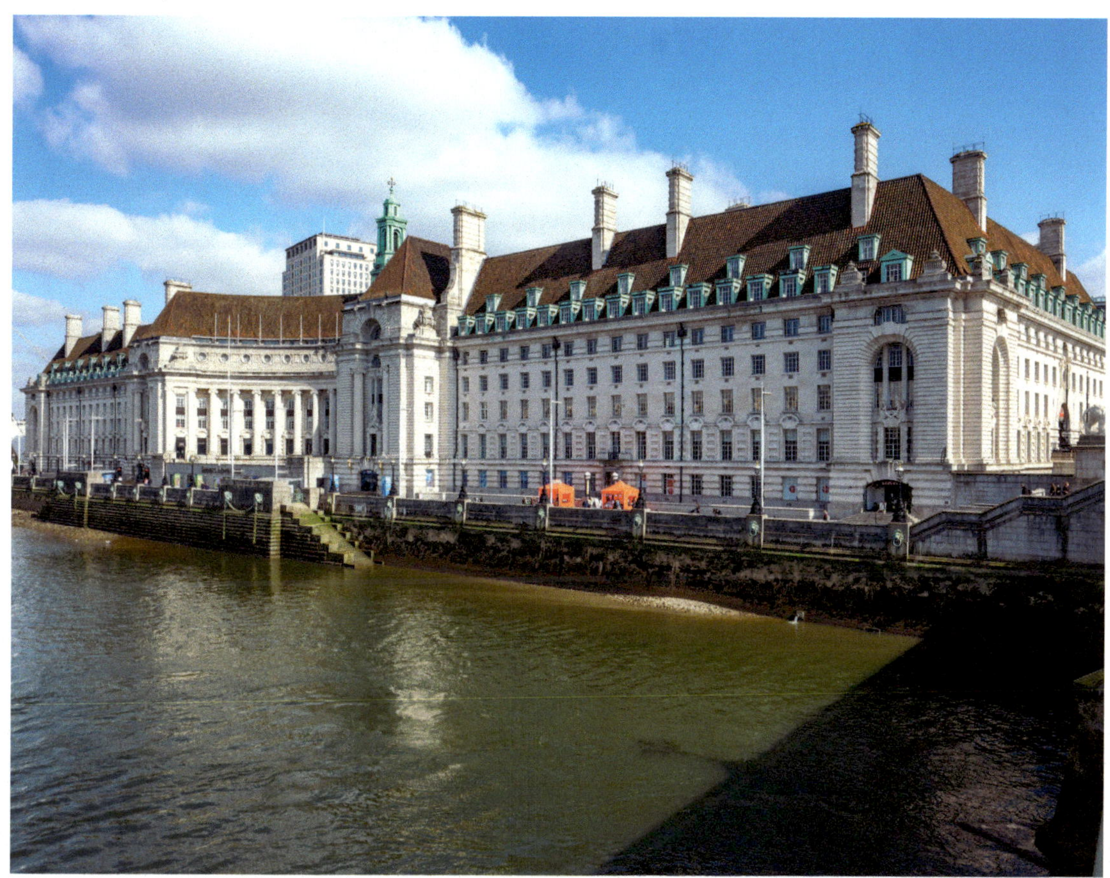

County Hall is proud of its provenance. Words in gold proclaim 'The Home of London Government from 1922 to 1986' and plaques on the south facing wall commemorate the LCC and GLC offices and the Inner London Education Authority, which had started life as the London School Board, surviving until 1990. Sculptures at the eastern end represent recreation, town planning, child education and care of the sick and above are eleven coats of arms representing London boroughs.

In 1988 the Marriott hotel opened within the main County Hall block.

Address: Westminster Bridge Road, SE1 7PB
Built: 1911/1922 – Ralph Knott; 1930s; 1974
Listed Status: Grade I
Public Access: Yes
Tube/Rail: Waterloo, Westminster
Website: marriott.com

11. London Eye

If one image has defined London's changing skyline since the millennium it would be the London Eye, the world's largest observation wheel. Formally opened on 31 December 1999 with Queen Elizabeth II as its first passenger, public 'flights' began on 9 March 2000. Originally considered a blight on London's south bank and tolerated only as a temporary structure celebrating the year 2000, it almost immediately became a much-loved visitor attraction. Despite changing sponsors and several rebrandings the official name has never changed.

Husband and wife architectural team Marks Barfield were the designers and the project was underway by 1993 with Julia Barfield suggesting the site near County Hall (see Entry 10), the circular wheel motif referencing the 1951 Festival of Britain's Dome of Discovery (see Box) and support from British Airways, hence the notion of a flight, sealed the project. The wheel is 135 metres tall with a diameter of 120 metres. Weighing 600 tons, it was transported via the River Thames, lying horizontal until raised into position, the largest object ever to be lifted in that manner.

The thirty-two capsules or pods, representing the thirty-two London boroughs (minus the City of London) number from one to thirty-three with thirteen omitted. Each pod can hold twenty-five passengers and a flight takes thirty minutes with views as far as 40 km on a clear day.

The legacy of the London Eye reverberates throughout the neighbourhood, as Marks Barfield stipulated that 1 per cent of ticket revenue should be used for local community projects.

Address: Riverside Building, County Hall, SE1 7PB
Built: 1999 – Marks Barfield
Public Access: Yes
Tube/Rail: Waterloo, Westminster
Website: londoneye.com

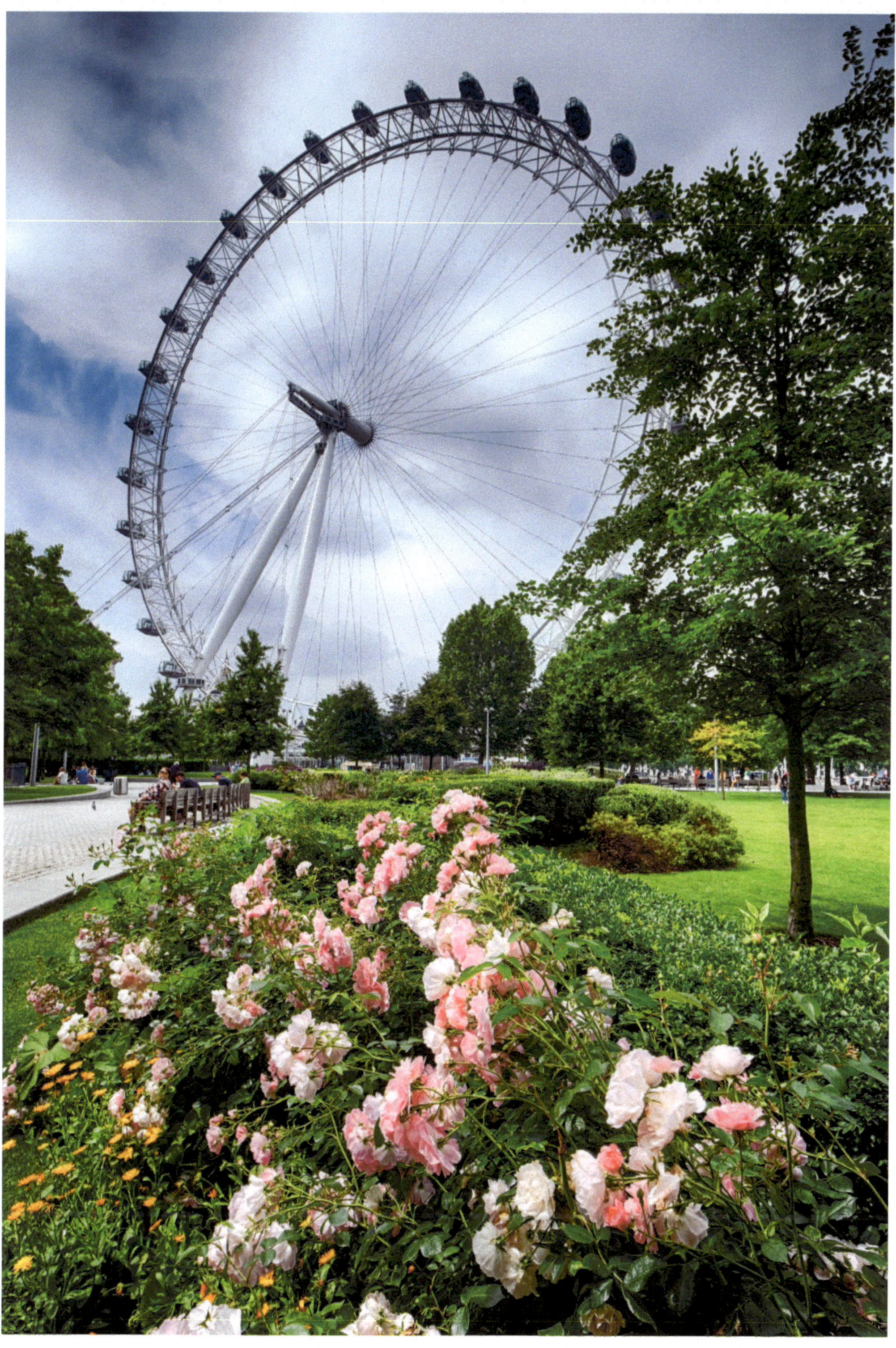

London Eye from Jubilee Gardens.

The Festival of Britain

The riverside walkway commemorates the Festival of Britain held between May and October 1951. Only the Royal Festival Hall (see Entry 13) survived intact as other festival structures, including the Dome of Discovery, were swiftly dismantled. Soaring into the sky flying the Union Flag is the 20-metre-high wooden flagpole gifted to the festival by the timber trade of British Columbia and resited here in 1977 commemorating Queen Elizabeth II's Silver Jubilee. Near its base a circular brass strip commemorates The Skylon. Designed by Powell & Moya, the slender cigar-shaped structure, over 90 metres tall, became an iconic symbol of the festival. Alongside is a colourful carousel, a 1999 replica of the one in Battersea Park Festival Gardens. For more information and artefacts see the display in the Royal Festival Hall foyer.

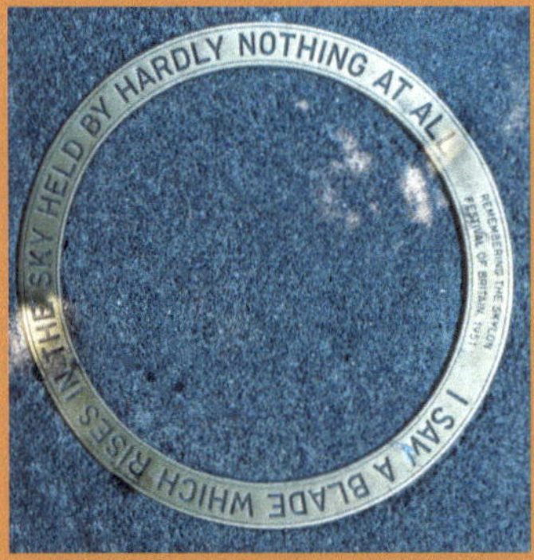

Skylon plaque.

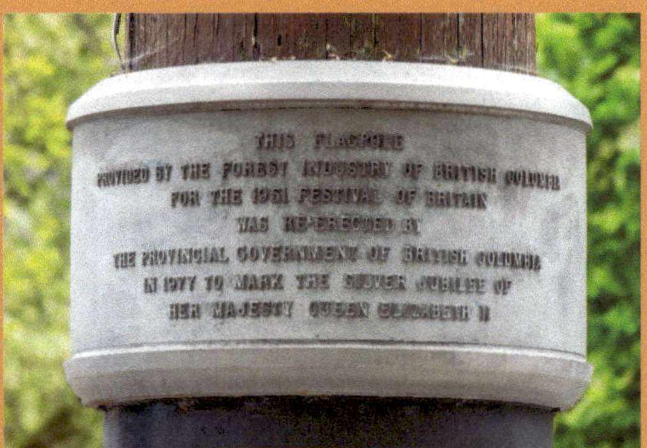

Flagpole.

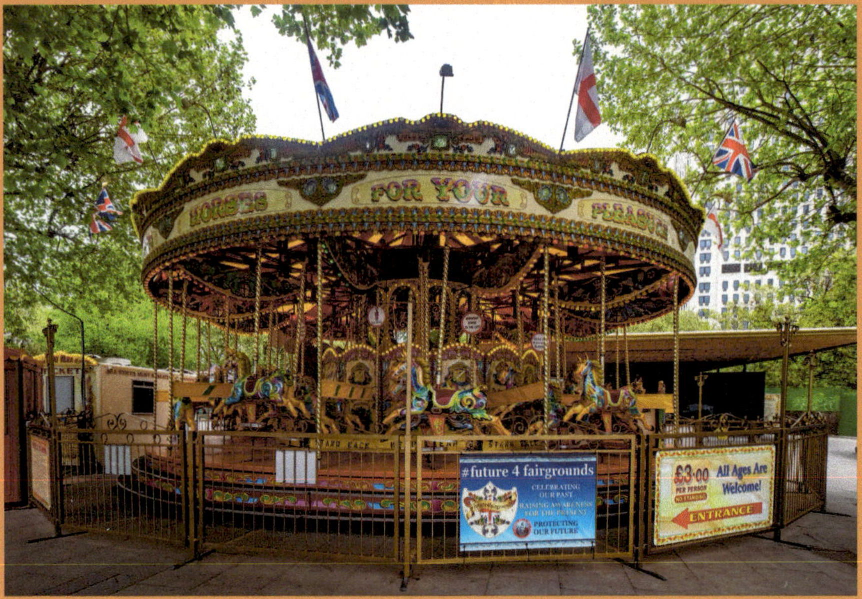

Carousel.

12. Shell Centre

Dominating the south side of Jubilee Gardens and commissioned in 1962 as the London Headquarters for Royal Dutch Shell, this imposing twenty-seven-storey tower occupies part of the land cleared for the 1951 Festival of Britain. Created between 1957 and 1962, it was part of an LCC initiative revitalising the neighbourhood.

The Shell building with its slab-sided Portland stone structure and flush bronze-framed windows of Burma teak referenced the New York skyline, where architect Sir Howard Robertson had been involved with the design of the United Nations Headquarters.

When built, the Shell Centre was London's largest and tallest office building and comprised the central tower with three nine-storey wings. It contained an Olympic-sized

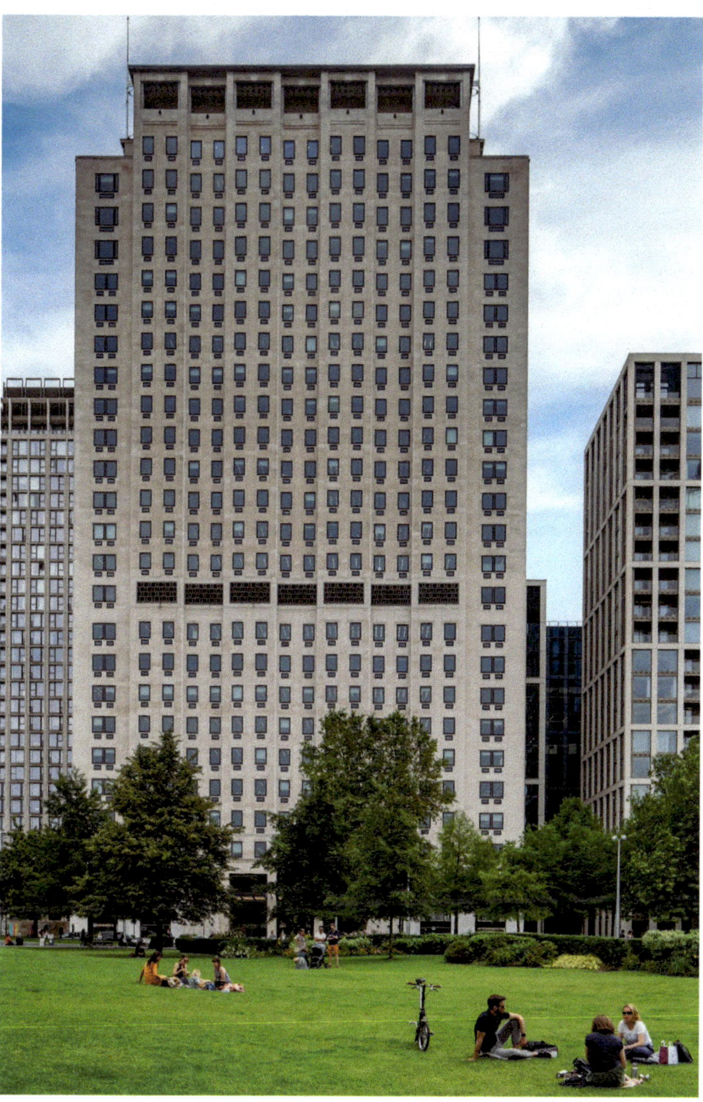

The Shell Centre.

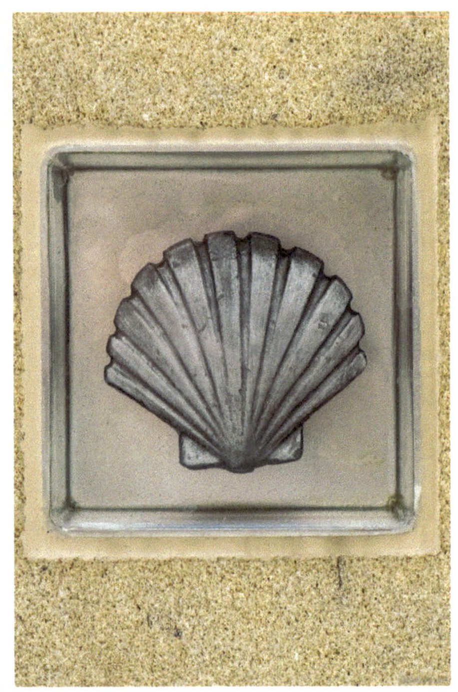

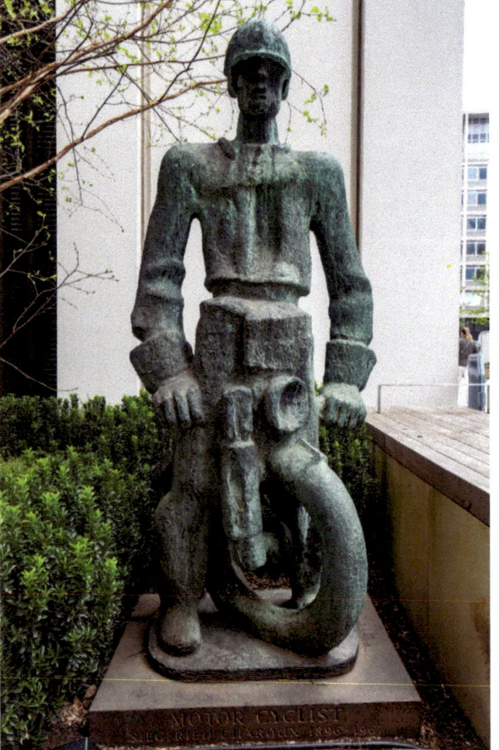

Above left: *Wave* Shell sculpture above the main entrance.

Above right: Familiar Shell Petroleum logo inset to the benches.

Left: *Motor Cyclist* by Siegfried Charoux.

swimming pool, squash courts, a rifle range, its own telephone exchange, shops and a theatre. The interior was decorated to a very high standard and commissioned sculptures enhanced the surrounding landscape. At one time a public viewing gallery occupied the top floor. The recent redevelopment to a master plan by Squires and Partners included the removal of the three adjacent wings. In their place five blocks provide offices, retail outlets and 858 homes, with three named after Hugh Casson, project leader for the Festival of Britain. Sculpted shells salvaged from previous buildings are embedded above entrances and within new public benches. A new walkway is home to the relocated *Motorcyclist* sculpture by Siegfried Charoux.

A second Shell block designed by Robertson was built on the other side of the Hungerford Bridge. Known as the Downstream building to differentiate it from the other blocks known as the Upstream, it remains intact opposite the Royal Festival Hall's south elevation.

Address: Southbank Place, York Road, SE1 7LZ
Built: 1957/1962 – Sir Howard Robertson; 2017/2022 – Squire and Partners
Listed Status: Grade II (Fountain)
Public Access: No
Tube/Rail: Waterloo

13. Royal Festival Hall

The Royal Festival Hall (RFH) is the only survivor of the 1951 Festival of Britain and the first post-Second World War building to be Grade I listed. It was planned independently of the festival to replace the Queen's Hall in Marylebone, destroyed in 1941.

Lead architects Leslie Martin and Peter Moro, based next door at County Hall (see Entry 10), had three years to design and build a flagship concert hall. The monumental river frontage is both solid and glazed allowing passersby to peek inm with the parabolic roof indicating the auditorium within. In the early 1960s the main entrance was relocated from the ground level at the north-east to the riverside via an upper walkway.

The interior remains a feat of engineering design. The performance space is an 'egg in a box' with the concert hall above the foyer cushioned against any potential movement from trains by bars, lecture spaces and restaurants. The expansive foyer's raked ceiling is the underside of the auditorium. The staircases have cantilevered half-landings and only appear to be connected to adjacent pillars. The result is a public space enabling different vantage points and panoramic views across the river. The carpet designed by Moro as a visual interpretation of sound waves incorporates a solid blob added by Martin. Known as *Net and Ball,* it has became one of the most enduring post-Second World War designs. The bars were available to everyone and the GLC's Open Door policy of the early 1980s opened up the RFH to the public during the day. The RFH entices passers-by to enter and exit from different levels and doorways, each with different visuals attracting the eye. Entering from the riverside reveals a display of Festival of Britain artefacts and outside the upper western level is a bust of anti-apartheid campaigner Nelson Mandela. Outside the ground level eastern entrance is a sculpture commemorating Polish musician Frédéric Chopin.

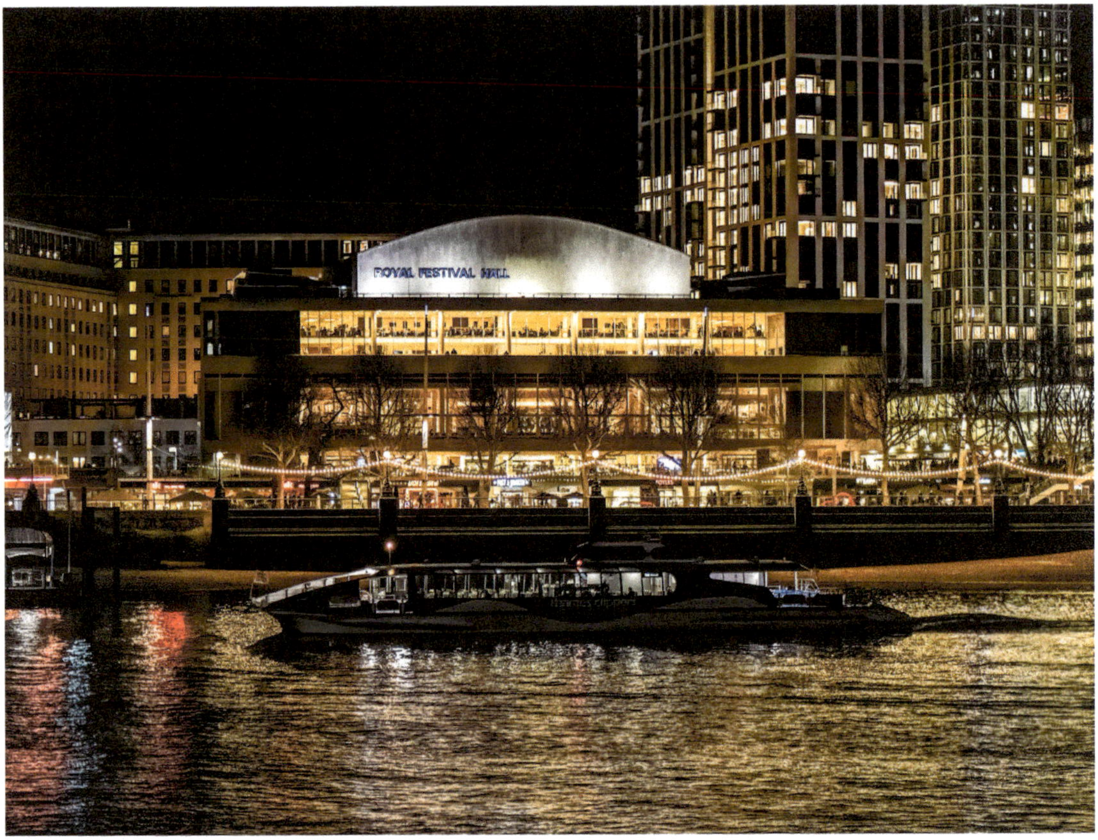

Above and below: Royal Festival Hall.

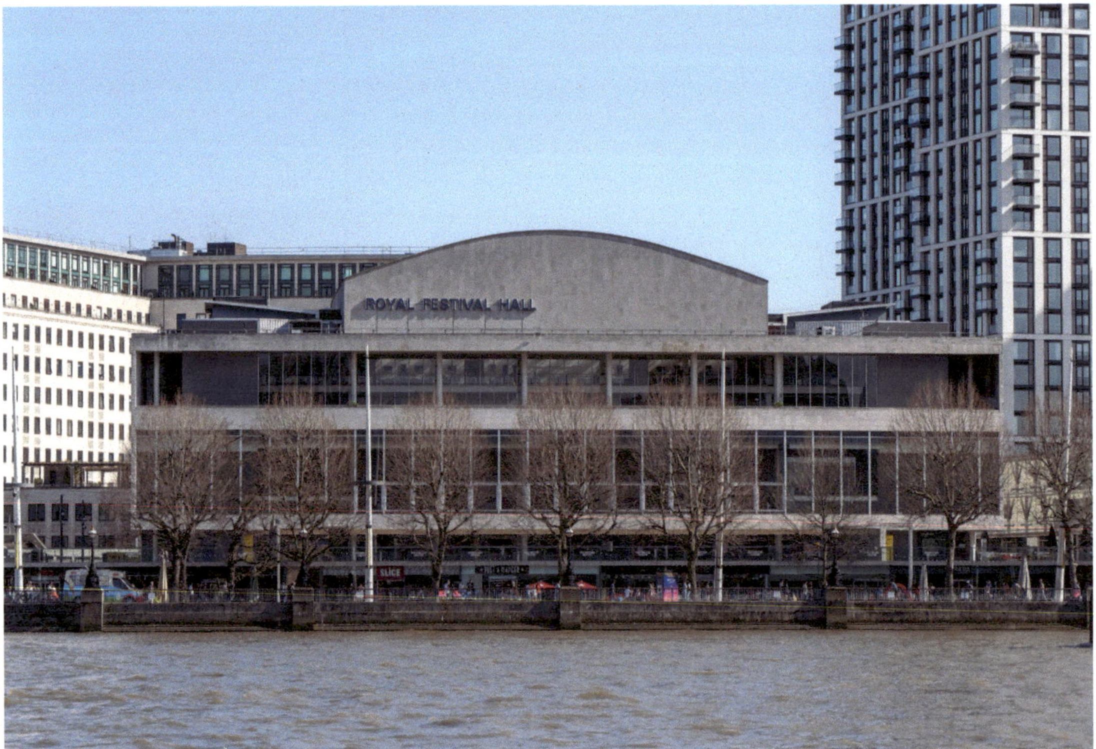

The RFH, one of the three performance venues comprising the Southbank Centre, hosts the best of classical, world, jazz and folk music, ballroom and world dance, the annual Women of the World festival, film premieres and literary events.

Address: Southbank Centre, Belvedere Road, SE1 8XX
Built: 1951 – Leslie Martin, Robert Matthew, Peter Moro; refurbishment 2004/07 – Allies & Morrison
Listed Status: Grade I
Public Access: Yes
Tube/Rail: Waterloo
Website: southbankcentre.co.uk

14. Queen Elizabeth Hall and Hayward Gallery

The Queen Elizabeth Hall (QEH) and Hayward Gallery are often overlooked, despite bright yellow staircases alongside. Following the Festival of Britain the pavilions were swiftly demolished with only the Royal Festival Hall (see Entry 13) remaining, isolated amid a new urban wilderness, but its success had fuelled an appetite for new cultural experiences and, in response, plans were made for an additional concert hall and an art gallery. LCC architect Norman Engleback worked in collaboration with the Arts Council, engineers, designers and performers to produce buildings where the needs of the performers and gallery spaces were paramount and the building opened in 1967. The grey exterior comprises Cornish granite panels with delightful detailing, with Baltic pine moulds for the concrete providing a delicately ridged texture. The interior floors are marble and sizeable windows allowed passers-by to see inside. Incorporated in 1967 was an additional smaller performance space, the Purcell Room, named after seventeenth-century composer Henry Purcell.

Musical performances traverse classical to folk, contemporary to jazz and rock to electronic and opportunities abound for audiences to enjoy emerging artists and composers. The spoken word is showcased through events such as Poetry International, initiated in 1967 soon after the complex opened.

The undercroft had been designed as an empty space but became an informal skateboarding arena in the 1970s, bringing a unique form of entertainment for passers-by and they honed their skills alongside a colourful backdrop by graffiti artists. Plans unveiled in 2013 for a revamp of the SBC included the relocation of the skateboard park but it was saved following a vociferous public campaign. The refurbished QEH reopened in 2018.

The Hayward Gallery dating from 1968 is named after Sir Isaac Hayward, LCC Chair between 1947 and its abolition in 1965.

However, it proved difficult for the public to find and in 1972 the UK's first public kinetic sculpture was unveiled above the roofline to attract visitors.

The neon-lit 14-metre-high tower seemed to move and rotate while also changing colour and the designers and public alike were disappointed when, in 2008, the tower was removed for renovation and never reinstalled. The pedestrian area outside is now used an external exhibition space showcasing artists championed by the Hayward. With no

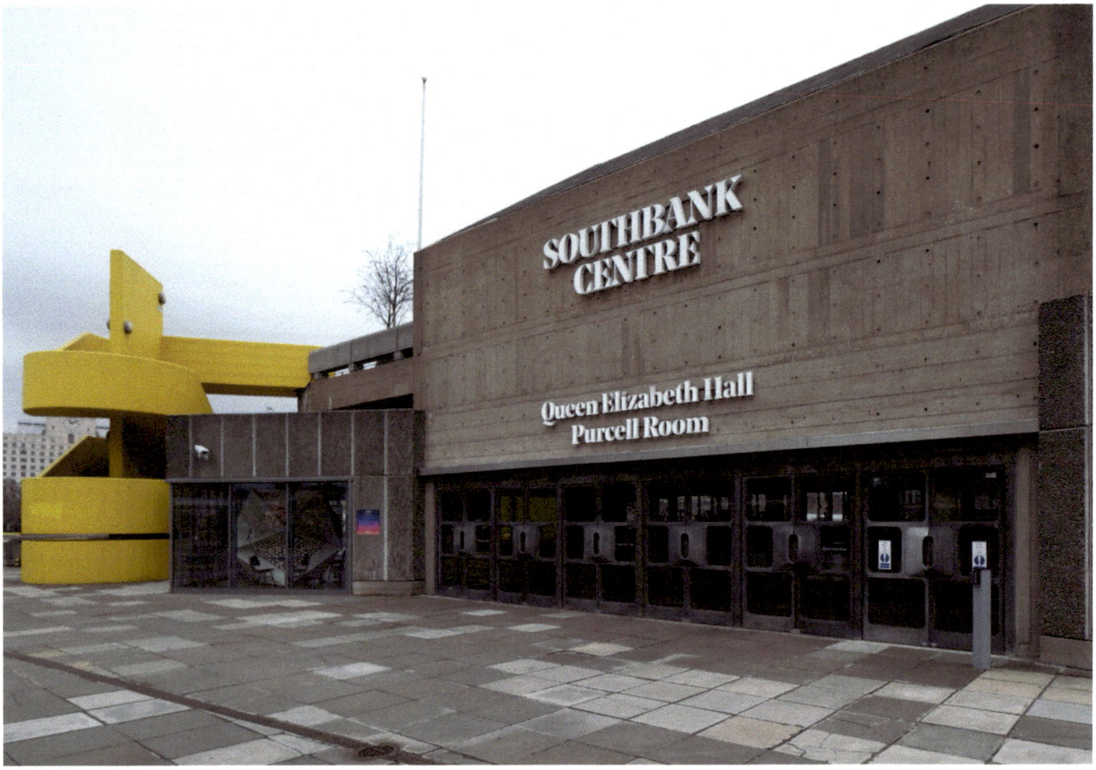

Above: Queen Elizabeth Hall.

Below: Hayward Gallery.

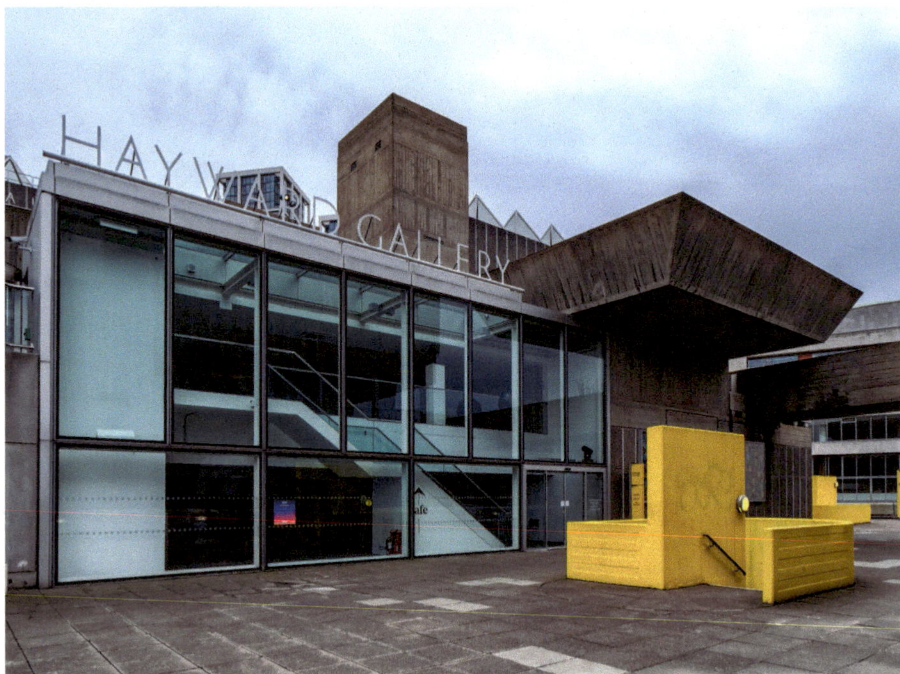

permanent collection of its own the gallery showcases the best of twentieth-century art through temporary exhibitions.

Refurbishment in 2003 introduced a large glass-fronted foyer and during the mid-2010s the sixty-five rooftop steel and glass pyramids were renovated, becoming a new iconic Hayward feature.

Address: Southbank Centre, Belvedere Road, SE1 8XX
Built: QEH – 1963/67; Hayward Gallery – 1963/68 – both Norman Engleback
Public Access: Yes
Tube/Rail: Waterloo
Website: southbankcentre.co.uk

15. BFI Southbank

While not in its original location, BFI Southbank is the only remaining feature from the Festival of Britain, other than the RFH (see Entry 13). Access to the complex is through the modern glass-sided steel extension off Belvedere Road or via the riverside bar beneath Waterloo Bridge.

Its origin lies in the Telekinema (also spelt Telecinema), built to show both film and TV programmes. Designed by Wells Coates, the projection booth was visible through glass allowing visitors to see film and sound equipment in action. Films included 35 mm, stereophonic, stereoscopic and experimental 3D. Originally located further north, the cinema was moved to the Riverside Restaurant site after the festival closed.

Below and overleaf: BFI Southbank.

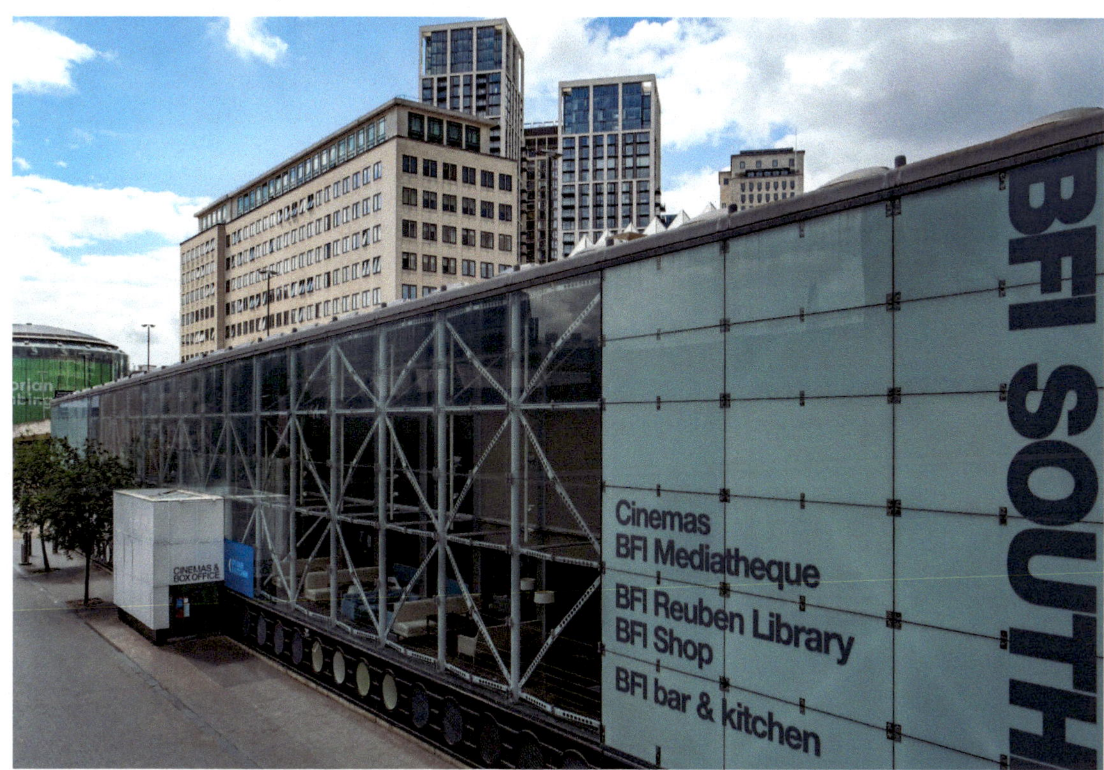

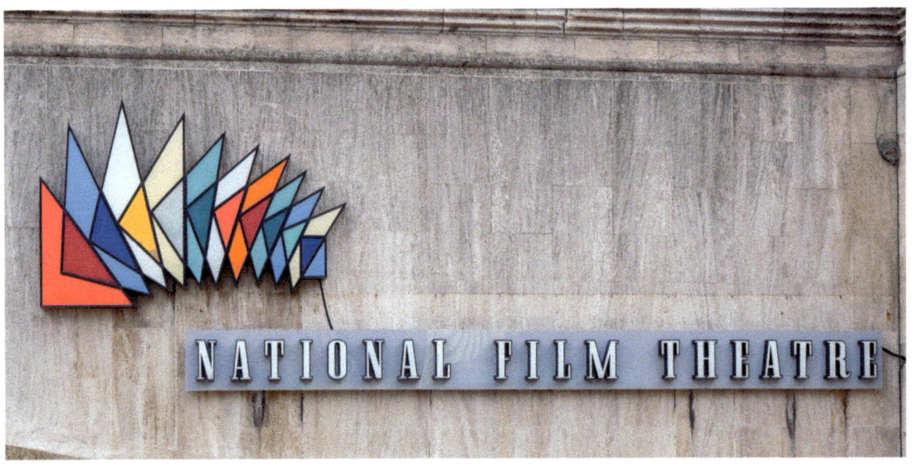

In 1952, the BFI (British Film Institute) took over the cinema, renaming it the National Film Theatre (NFT). The building was closed in 1957, was rebuilt and later rebranded as BFI Southbank in 2007. A brightly coloured sign on the western elevation of Waterloo Bridge is the only external remaining NFT signage. Further change came when structures previously used for MOMI (Museum of Moving Image), a much loved but short-lived visitor attraction between 1988 and 1999, were incorporated into the complex.

BFI Southbank retained the cinema names NFT1 and NFT2 and, with the extra space from MOMI, opened an additional cinema, NFT3, in 2007, plus a small thirty-eight-seater, The Studio, the same year.

In 2022 the reworked riverside exterior with a bold fibreglass canopy below Waterloo Bridge won a RIBA architecture award. In addition to the four cinemas, BFI Southbank houses the BFI Reuben Library, the Mediateque for viewing BFI Archive films and a Mezzanine Gallery for temporary exhibitions and eating and drinking facilities.

Address: Belvedere Road, SE1 8XT
Built: 1957 – Norman Engleback; 2007 – Buchanan Hartley Architects; 2022 – Carmody Groarke
Public Access: Yes
Tube/Rail: Waterloo
Website: BFI.org.uk

16. Royal National Theatre

On its opening in 1976 the National Theatre (from 1990 the Royal National Theatre), designed by Denys Lasdun, divided both theatregoers and architectural critics. Labelled variously a brutalist monster, a fortress and a nuclear power station, this concrete addition to the South Bank gave way to a surprisingly warm and relaxing interior.

London had been awaiting its new theatre since 1963 when Sir Laurence Olivier established his National Theatre Company, with the fledgling company performing at the Old Vic while the new theatre was constructed. The lightly coloured concrete complements

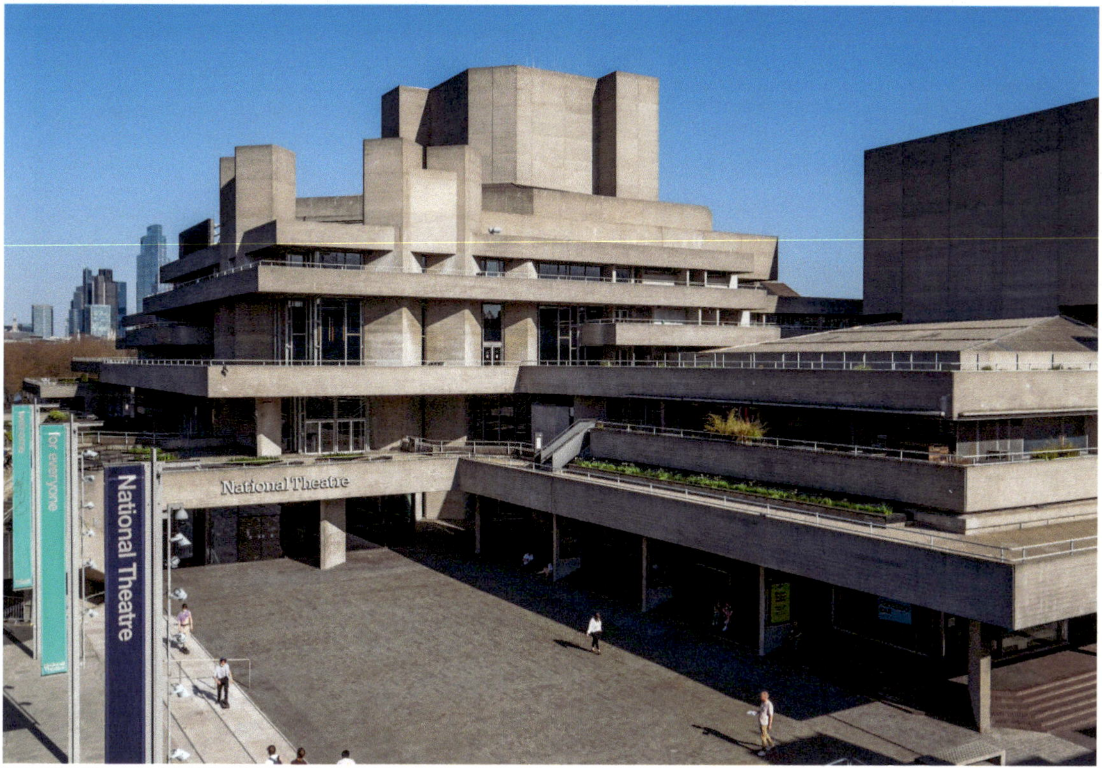

Above: Royal National Theatre.

Below: *London Pride* by Frank Dobson.

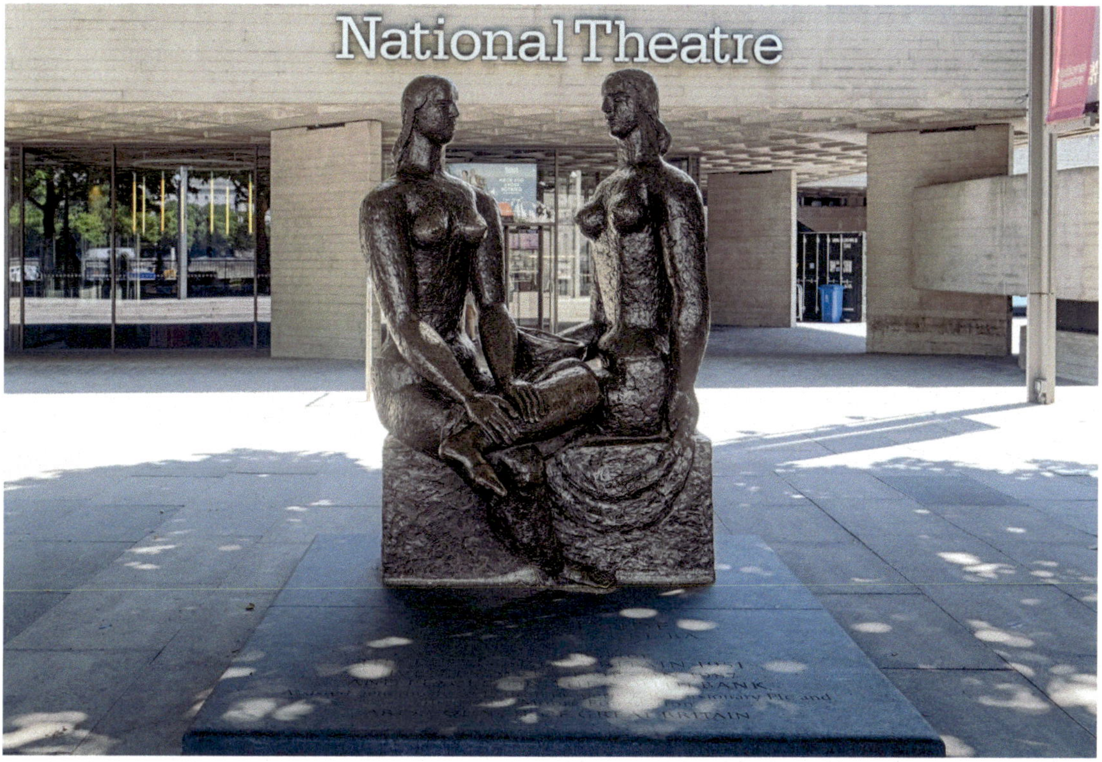

the Portland stone of Waterloo Bridge alongside and Somerset House on the north bank. Two fly towers, linked by different sized storeys and roof terraces, ensured that the view of the theatre was different from each angle. Peter Hall, its first artistic director, had three performance spaces to programme.

The largest, the Olivier Theatre, is in classic open theatre style, the Lyttleton named after Oliver Lyttleton, the National Theatre's first Chair, has a traditional proscenium stage, and the smaller Cottesloe, for experimental productions, opened in 1977 with a separate exterior entrance. It commemorated Lord Cottesloe, then Chairman of the South Bank. The two main theatres are linked by carpeted foyers and soft lighting ensured the public space never felt frenetic. Public exhibitions linked to the performing arts were displayed regularly and the acoustics allowed for personal conversations amid general foyer hullaballoo. This contrast between exterior and interior proved key to the theatre's success.

London Pride by Frank Dobson, a sculpture commissioned for the Festival of Britain, was returned to the south bank in 1987 and positioned outside the NT facing the Thames. During 1997/2000 renovations, the vehicle riverfront road was transformed into a pedestrianised walkway, welcoming in 2007 a sculpture depicting Sir Laurence Olivier as Hamlet.

In 2014 the Cottesloe became the Dorfman Theatre, a workshop space, honouring Lloyd Dorfman, the founder of Travelex who initiated a scheme for low-cost theatre tickets. In the same year the Clore Learning Centre, providing workshop and event spaces, opened.

Address: Upper Ground, SE1 9PX
Built: 1969/76 – Denys Lasdun; 1997/2000 – Stanton Williams
Listed Status: Grade II*
Public Access: Yes
Tube/Rail: Southwark, Waterloo
Website: nationaltheatre.org.uk

17. Royal Waterloo Hospital

The ornate red brick and terracotta building on the corner of Stamford Street is currently student accommodation for the University of Notre Dame (USA) London campus, and between 1981 and 2011 it housed Schiller International University students. However, the fascia alongside Waterloo Bridge proclaiming The Royal Waterloo Hospital for Children and Women signals its original purpose. Built between 1903/05, it replaced a previous hospital on the same site built in 1822 and extended several times throughout the 1800s. Originating in 1816 as the Universal Dispensary for Children at Blackfriars, patronage from King George III's children added Royal to its name, with branches established throughout London. A new site was found at the southern end of Waterloo Bridge, a rapidly developing area since the bridge opened in 1817. Eventually, in 1875, following more name changes and bequests the hospital became the Royal Hospital for Children and Women, with Waterloo added in 1903. The hospital continued to grow through the twentieth century with a nurses' home opening in 1927 on York Road. Incorporated into the NHS in 1948, the hospital closed in 1976.

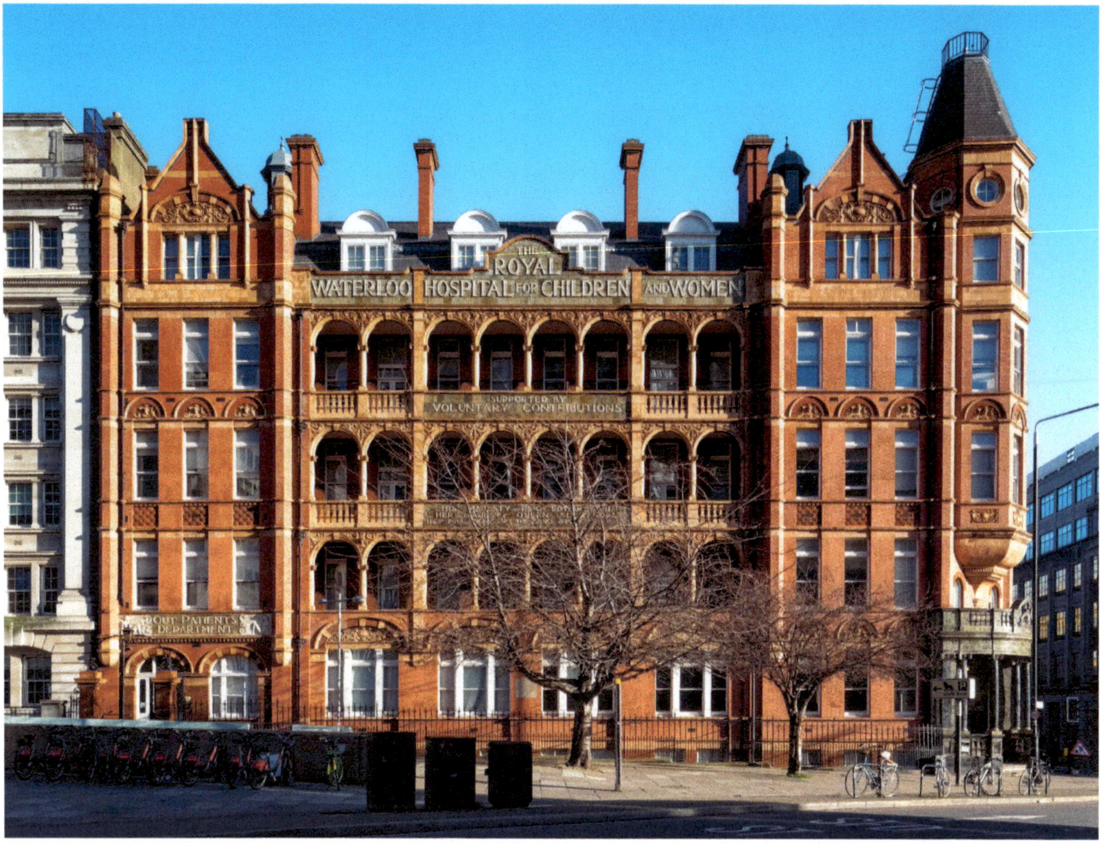

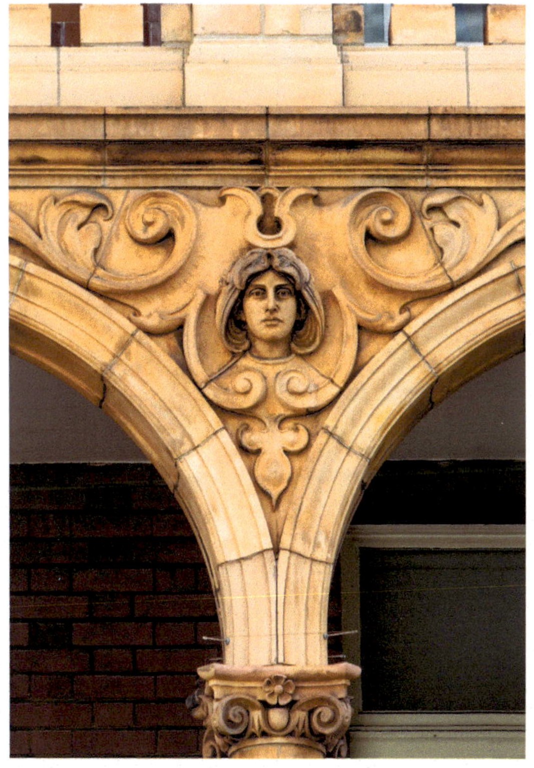

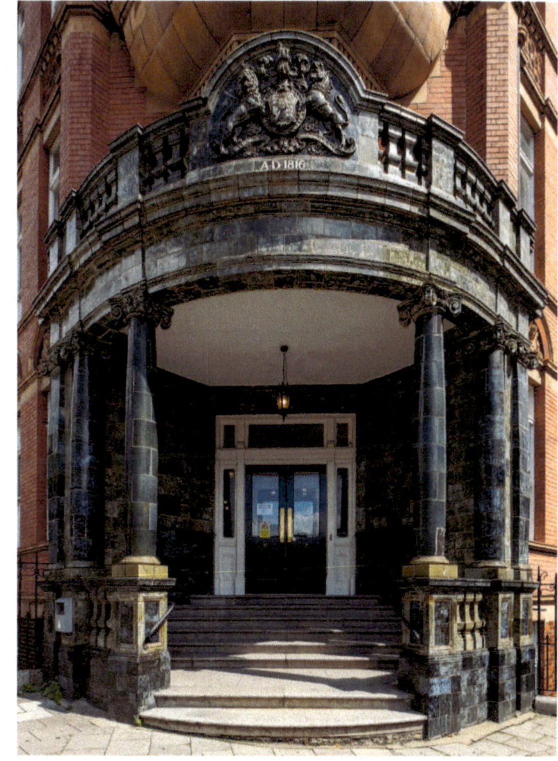

Above and below left and below right: Royal Waterloo Hospital for Women and Children.

The foundation stone on Waterloo Bridge Road was laid by the Duchess of Albany, Queen Victoria's daughter-in-law, and the corner entrance turret bearing a royal insignia is lined with blue and turquoise glazed tiles, a gift from Henry Doulton whose ceramics factory was nearby (see Entry 3).

Address: Waterloo Bridge Road, SE1 8TX
Built: 1903/05 – M. S. Nicholson
Listed Status: Grade II
Public Access: No
Tube/Rail: Waterloo

18. Waterloo Station Victory Arch

The 1922 Victory Arch, serving as the main entrance to Waterloo station, commemorates the sacrifice in the First World War of 585 employees of the London & South Western Railway (LSWR). The arch is one of the largest war memorials of its type in London but is greatly overlooked by the millions of passengers who pass through it every year. Designed by James Robb Scott, chief architect to LSWR, the memorial is three storeys high with a central staircase rising from street level to the station concourse.

Above the date 1914 is Bellona, goddess of war, surrounded by four mourning figures. Opposite to the right, 1918 indicates the armistice, with Peace holding a small flag of victory surrounded by mourners including a baby.

Waterloo station Victory Arch.

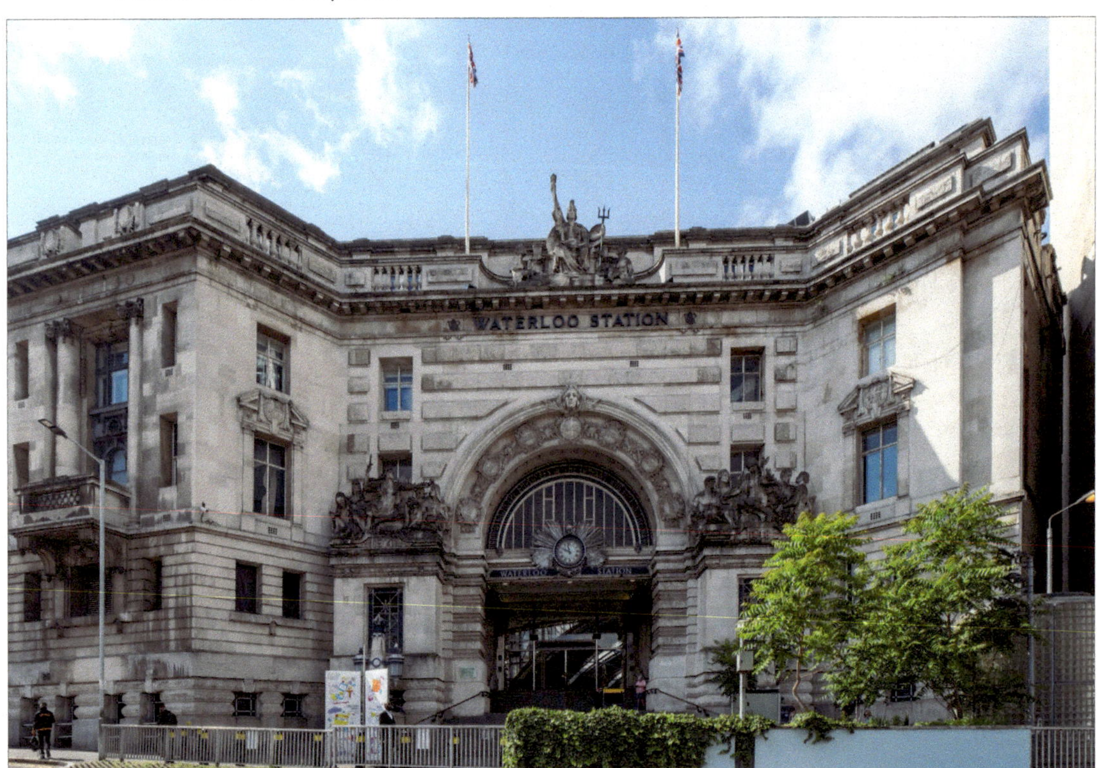

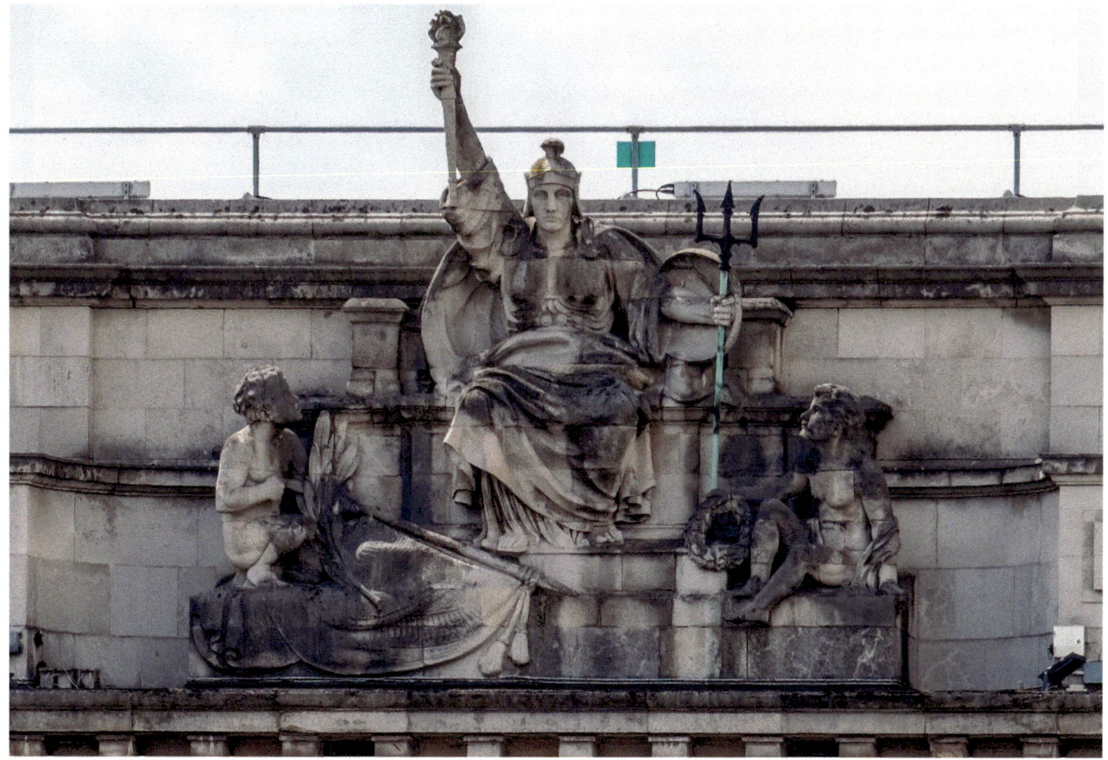

Britannia statue on top of the Victory Arch.

The main stone arch above features cartouches naming sea and land battles where the men served. Contained within the arch are four brass panels listing the names of those who died in the First World War. Later plaques list names from a later generation of employees who fought in the Second World. On top of the arch is Britannia on her throne holding a torch and trident. Alongside are two children, one holding an olive branch and lowered military flag, the other a memorial wreath.

Waterloo was a main terminal in the First World War for the transport of military personnel to the Western Front and beyond and soldiers returning wounded could be transported by tunnel to the nearby military hospital (see Entry 21). Unique to memorials of its genre is that LSWR staff were consulted on its design. It was opened in March 1922 by Queen Mary as part of the completion of a substantial remodelling of Waterloo making the arch the main entrance.

The area fronting the arch is included in plans for overhaul by LB Lambeth, with the current road configuration set to incorporate Victory Arch Square, an open public space facilitating easier appreciation of this important and poignant memorial.

Address: Waterloo Road, SE1 8SW
Built: 1922 – James Robb Scott
Listed Status: Grade II
Public Access: Yes
Tube/Rail: Waterloo

19. St John's Waterloo and Sculpture Garden

On emerging from Waterloo station towards Waterloo Bridge the skyline is dominated by the portico and spire of the Church of St John's Waterloo. One of four Lambeth churches, all in Greek Revival style built as 'Waterloo' churches celebrating victory in 1815, they served a rapidly growing population south of the river. Consecrated in 1824, St John's was designed by Francis Bedford, with advice from engineer John Rennie due to the close proximity of the river and swampy ground. As such the church is built on deep piling. Rectangular in shape, the church is fronted by a portico with six Doric columns below a pediment with a classical style spire.

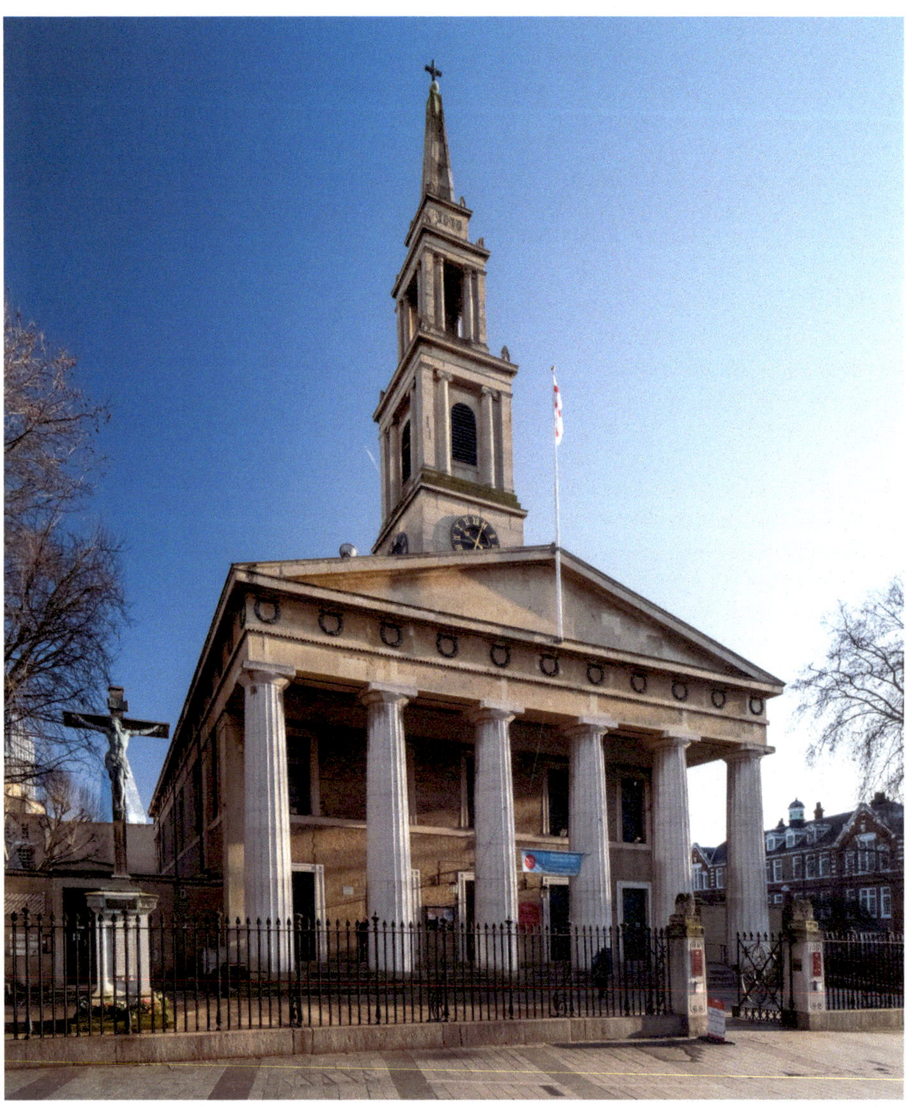

St John's Church, Waterloo.

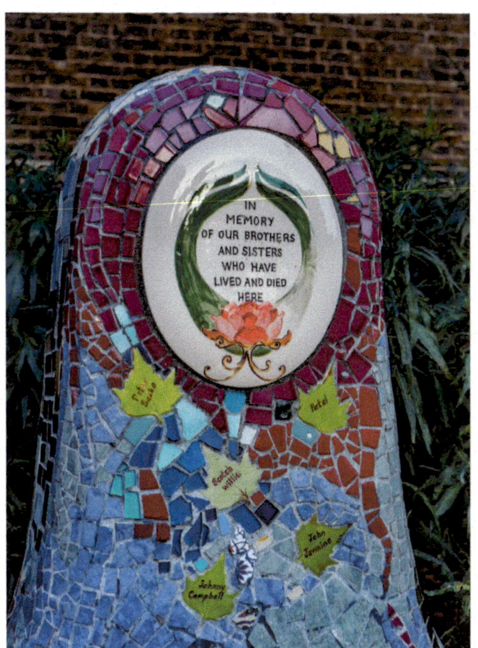

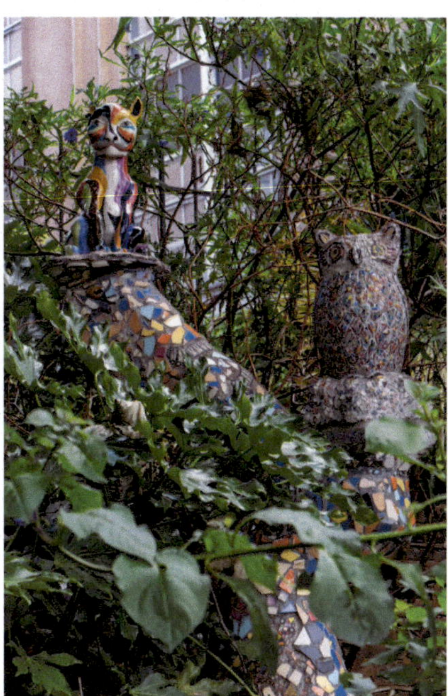

Above left: Mosaic memorial to the homeless.

Above right: Mosaic of The Owl and The Pussycat.

Right: Entrance to St John's churchyard.

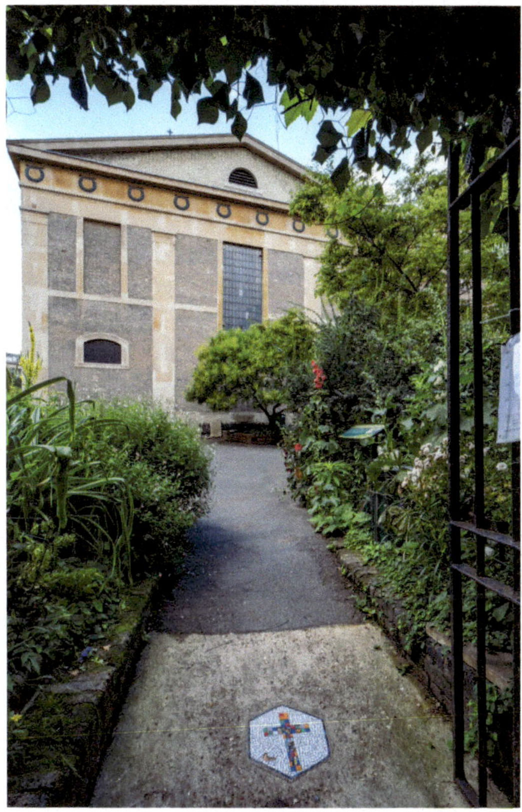

Renovated during the 1880s by Reginald Blomfield and internally by Sir Ninian Comper during 1924, the church was without its roof for ten years following damage during the Second World War. Two murals by emigre artist Hans Feibusch were commissioned and St John's reopened in time for the 1951 Festival of Britain. The churchyard, opened as a public garden in 1878 and now a lunchtime haven for local workers, contains a sculpture garden with artworks by Southbank Mosaics including a memorial bench commemorating homeless people who have died locally. A bench commemorating the bicentennial of Waterloo Bridge and the church's south elevation, seen from the garden, both include verse by seventeenth-century Welsh-born Anglican priest and poet George Herbert.

It is a vibrant parish serving a diverse community and The Creative Crypt is home to a number of social enterprises including artists' studios. Between July 2021 and the autumn of 2022, a £5 million renovation project transformed the semi-derelict crypt into a community space, restored the Feibusch murals, incorporated additional spaces for prayer and improved public access.

Address: No. 73 Waterloo Road, SE1 8TY
Built: 1824 – Francis Bedford; Refurbishment 2020s – Eric Parry
Listed Status: Grade II*
Public Access: Yes
Tube/Rail: Waterloo
Website: stjohnswaterloo.org

20. No. 127 Stamford Street

Stamford Street provides an alternative route between Waterloo and Blackfriars bridges. No. 127 Stamford Street was built by W. H. Smith & Son (WHS) as a printing works in 1915 for its rapidly growing range of services. The company derives its name from William Henry Smith, son of a newspaper distributor. He expanded the business into a UK-wide newspaper and magazine wholesaler and book publisher as well as building lucrative contracts for newsstands for the rapidly expanding Victorian railway network. By 1914 the company had over 4,000 employees and in addition to its print distribution services had moved into high street retail shops. It required printing, bookbinding and graphic design facilities for its own publications and those of its clients.

The large symmetrical four-storey building has a distinctly Egyptian flavour with the neo-Egyptian style of the distinctive tall recessed-niche glass windows reminiscent of the false-door architecture of ancient Egyptian tombs. The WHS logo includes a palm leaf motif and the stairwells have temple-like façades. It was designed by architect C. Stanley Peach, famous for the Centre Court at Wimbledon.

The building was sold by WHS to the *Telegraph* newspaper in 1939, which, due to the Second World War, never occupied it. Following war damage, it was subsequently used for storage. After renovation, it now provides student accommodation for King's College, London.

Address: No. 127 Stamford Street, SE1 9NQ
Built: 1915 – C Stanley Peach
Public Access: No
Tube/Rail: Southwark, Waterloo

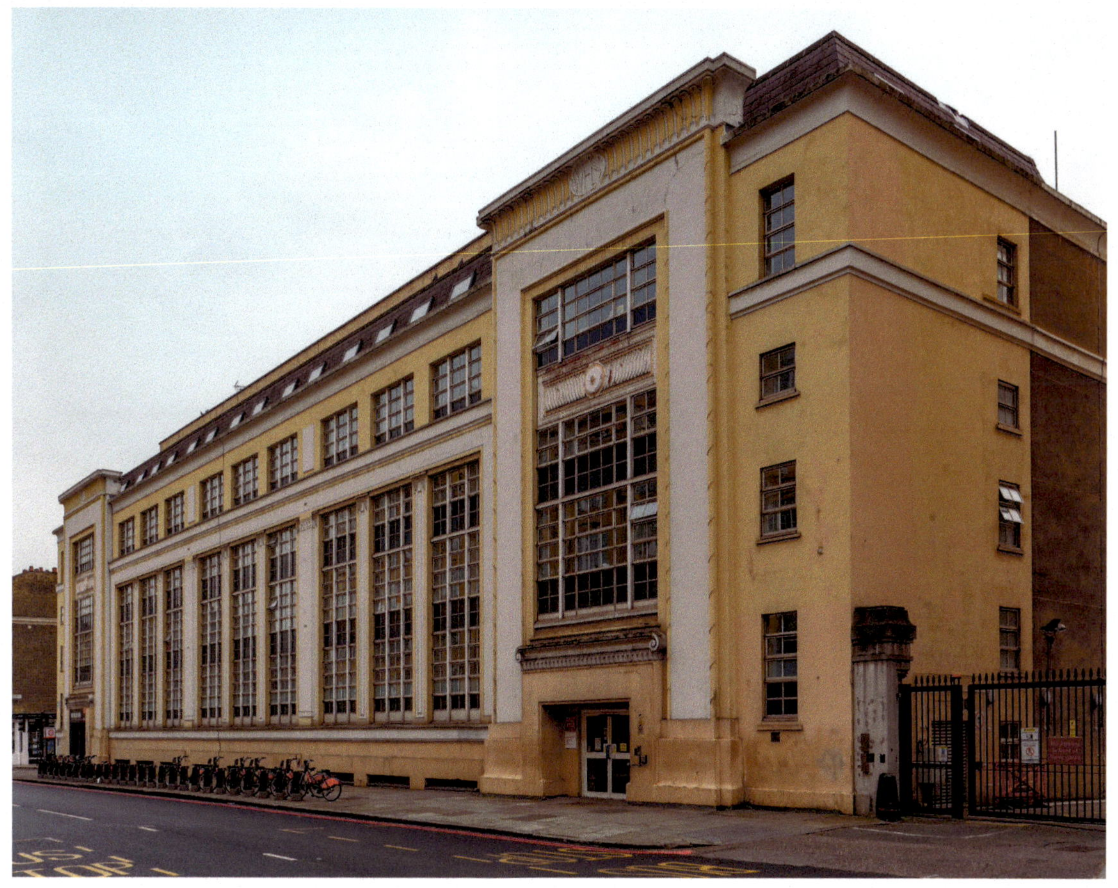

No. 127 Stamford Street, the former WHS Printing Works.

21. No. 150 Stamford Street

Opposite the WHS building (see Entry 20) another industrial building of a similar era and initially for the same function survives. A plain five-storey steel and concrete structure, it envelops the Hospital building (see Entry 17) as it continues to Waterloo Bridge Road. Opened in 1914 for His Majesty's Stationery Office (HMSO) as Cornwall House tunnels linked it to Waterloo station (see Entry 18), allowing easy passage for supplies and employees.

Completion of the building before the First World War created an important opportunity and it was swiftly commandeered and converted to the King George V Military Hospital. Funds raised by public subscription and support from the King and Queen Mary equipped the hospital with 1,650 beds and it was run jointly by the British Red Cross Society and Order of St John. From April 1915 the hospital received wounded military personnel from the Western Front, and later, from Gallipoli. Waterloo station was a key First World War transport link and the connecting tunnels were essential to bringing the wounded to the wards but also out of public gaze.

When the hospital closed in 1919 it had over 1,800 beds and had received 71,000 patients. In St John's (see Entry 19) stands a prominent crucifix, unveiled in 1917 and donated by the nursing staff as a memorial to patients who died at the hospital.

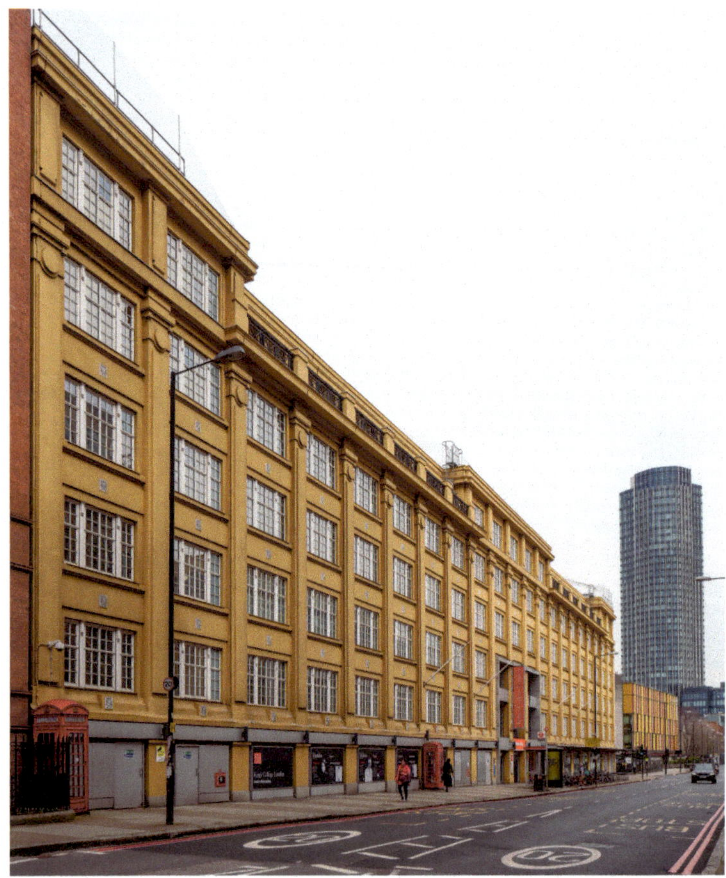

Franklin-Wilkins building.

It is now owned by King's College London. Renamed the Franklin-Wilkins building after Rosalind Franklin and Maurice Wilkins, who pursued their pioneering research into DNA at Kings' College, it houses cafés, the London Dental Education Centre and Franklin-Wilkins Library.

Address: No. 150 Stamford Street, SE1 9NH
Built: 1914
Public Access: No
Tube/Rail: Southwark, Waterloo

22. London Weekend Television

The tall square tower dominating the skyline on Upper Ground is officially The London Studios but known colloquially as London Weekend Tower. Over the decades other names have included The South Bank Studios, The London Television Centre, ITV Tower, LWT Tower and its original name Kent House, the only one that does not refer to the industry it was built for – television broadcasting. Opened in 1972 by the

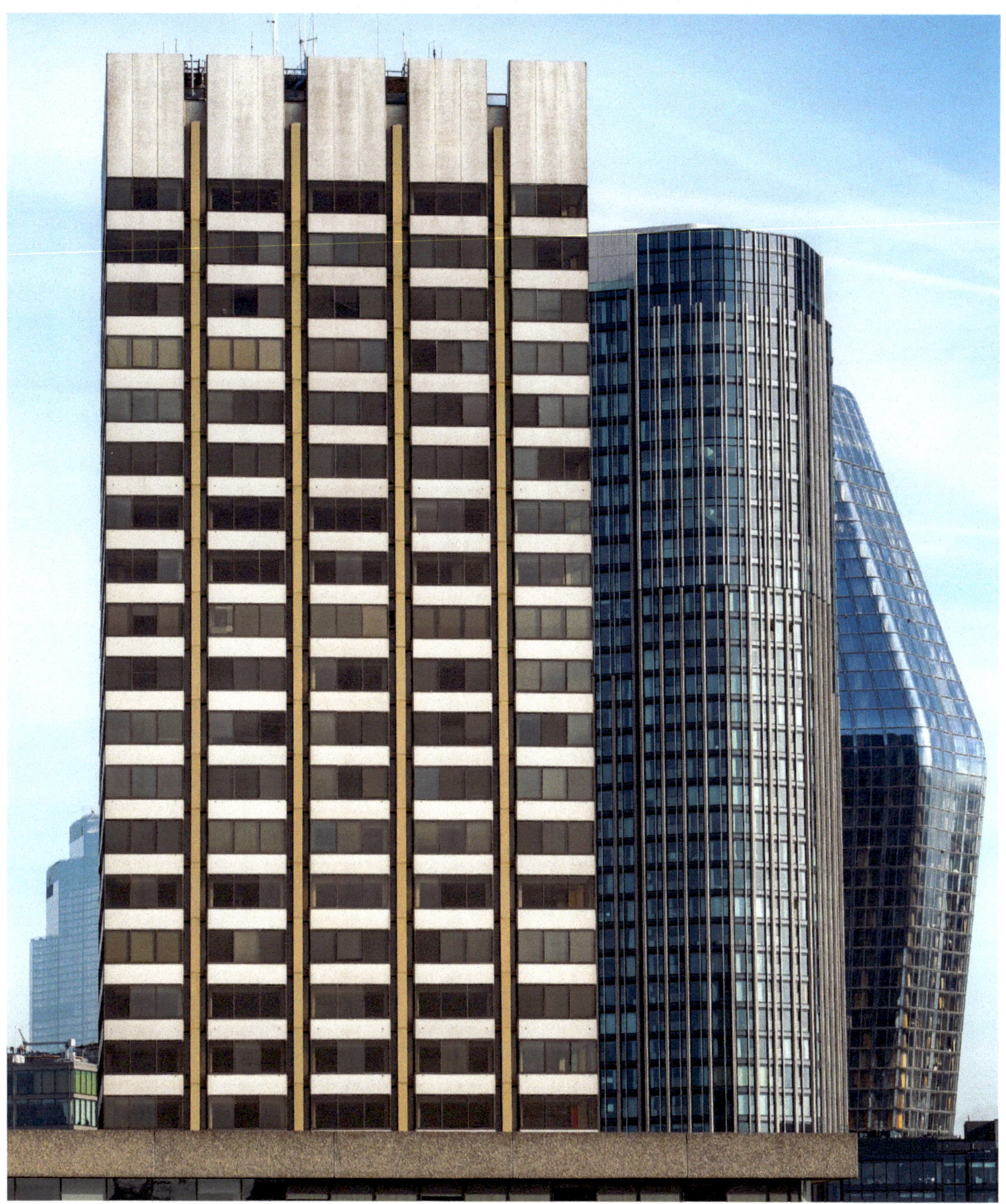

The LWT Tower and South Bank Cluster.

Duke of Kent, hence the name, the twenty-one-storey tower in a 2.5-acre site rises from a podium and was commissioned for London Weekend Television (LWT), the ITV (Independent TeleVision) franchise for Friday to Sunday programming. Designed by Elsom Pack & Roberts, it was one of Europe's most sophisticated broadcasting studios of its day.

LWT developed from the 1967 planned reorganisation of ITV franchises, which had a gap for weekends in London. LWT's offer included top broadcasters such as David Frost and programmes focussed on arts and social issues and broadcasting began from studios in Wembley, north-west London. With strikes during the launch week and audiences deserting the highbrow content, the response was swift with staff reorganisations, new funding and input from Rupert Murdoch. By 1971 LWT became key to Londoners' weekend viewing and the new headquarters and studios cemented the success. Into the 1980s additional scheduling catered for minority audiences and on a Saturday LWT programming kept Londoners happy between afternoon and early evening.

The building was the workplace for two twenty-one-time winners of the National Television Award for Best Presenter, Ant McPartlin and Declan Donnelly, better known as Ant and Dec. LWT became ITV1 in 2002 and the name disappeared from Britain's TV screens. The studios closed in 2018 and production relocated to the BBC Studioworks at White City, west London.

At time of writing the tower is awaiting demolition to be replaced by a twenty-six-storey office block.

Address: Upper Ground, SE1 9LT
Built: 1972 – Elsom and Partners (now EPR Architects)
Public Access: No
Tube/Rail: Southwark, Waterloo

23. Gabriel's Wharf

This delightfully ramshackle courtyard with eateries and independent retail outlets represents a David vs Goliath victory on the south bank. The site, originally a timber importing and retail company, was established in 1812 by sons of Christopher Gabriel, a late 1700s woodworking instrument maker. Renamed Gabriel's Wharf in 1815, following closure in 1919 the name was retained when various wharves and warehouses continued trading. Following the Second World War damage the area was left forlorn and neglected. With few employment opportunities the surrounding neighbourhood drastically depopulated from 50,000 to 4,000.

The 1970s witnessed the arrival of LWT, the National Theatre (see Entries 16 and 22) and IBM and developers began to re-evaluate the area with plans for a new riverside hotel and office blocks. But housing along Upper Ground would be cut off from river views and plunged into shadow. In response, the Coin Street Action Group (CSAG), named after a local street, was established.

The residents demanded cancellation of plans for the hotel and office blocks, plus more affordable housing, local shops and continued access to the river, and by 1984 campaigners

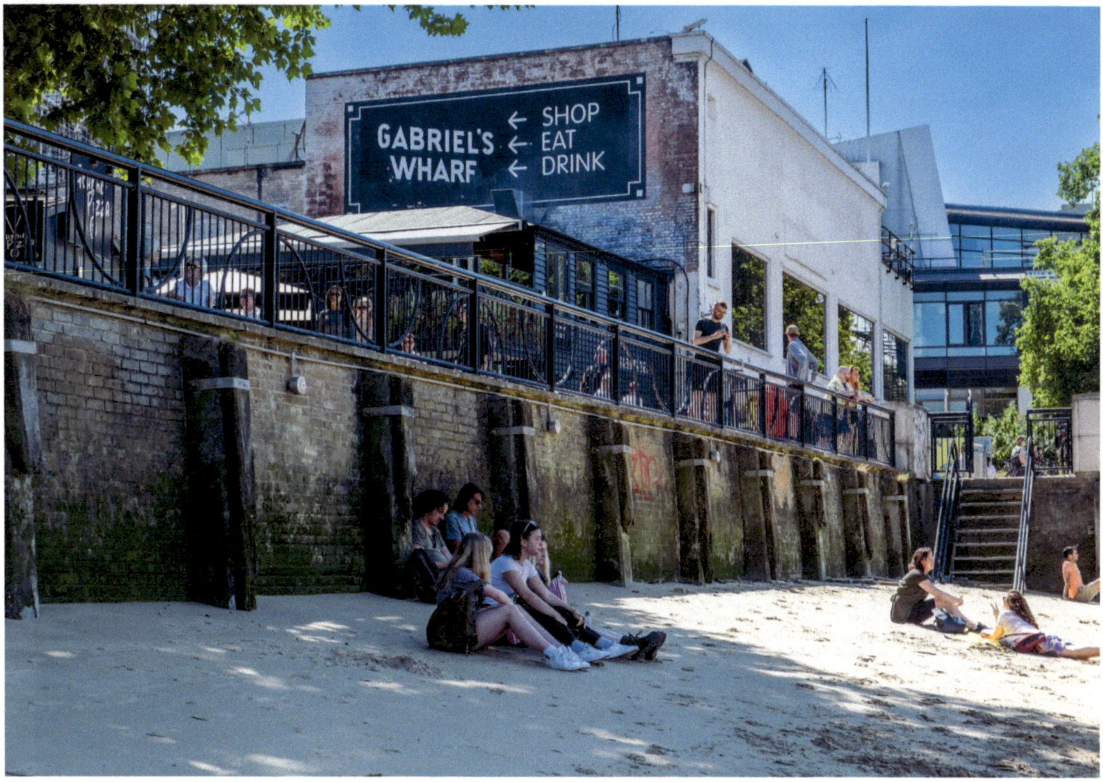

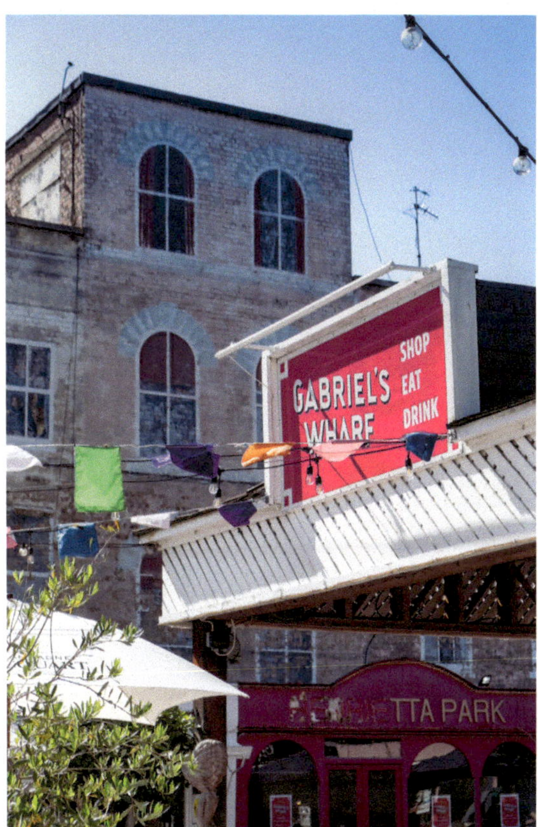

Above and below: Gabriel's Wharf and South Bank beach.

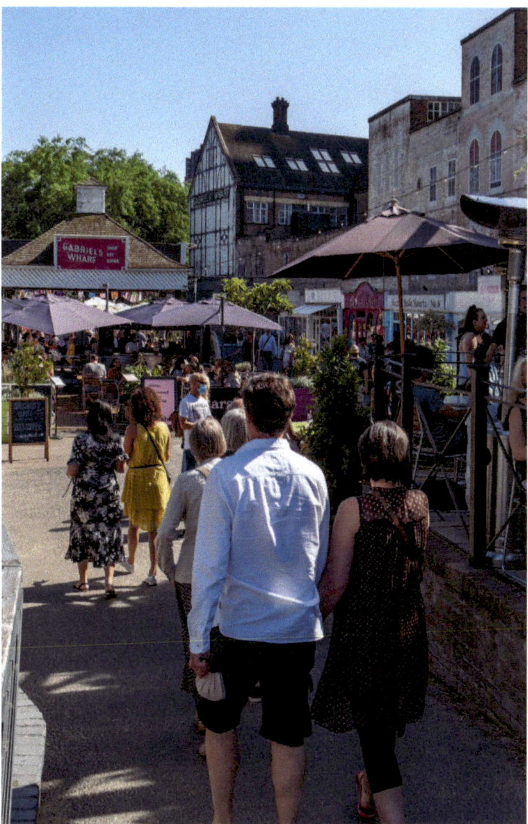

had formed Coin Street Community Builders (CSCB), acquired the land, destroyed mid-twentieth-century offices and designed landscaped riverside gardens, named to honour Bernadette Spain, an early campaigner.

The activists also seized control of the Oxo Tower (see Entry 24) and began transforming Gabriel's Wharf, then dominated by a cash 'n' carry warehouse and garages. Brightly coloured walls were still an unusual sight in the 1980s and upper storeys decorated with tromp d'oeil windows resembled homes above the shop fronts. In 1988 the enclave of small shops and restaurants around a courtyard with a makeshift bandstand opened to live music and open-air dancing.

To the rear, No. 58 Upper Ground, a 1930s mock-Tudor building, backs onto the Wharf leading to disused LWT studios and scenery workshops. Vacant since 2018, the site is currently awaiting redevelopment.

At the riverside, Ernie's Beach commemorates another local activist and founder member of CSAG, John Hearn (Ernie), a 1970s resident.

Address: Upper Ground, SE1 9PP
Built: Unknown
Public Access: Yes
Tube/Rail: Southwark, Waterloo
Website: coinstreet.org/gabriels-wharf

24. Oxo Tower

Sandwiched between Gabriel's Wharf (see Entry 23) and Sea Containers London Hotel (see Entry 26) the Oxo Tower is famous for clever use of glazing in the tower windows. Built as an electricity power station for the Royal Mail in the late nineteenth century, it was acquired in 1927 by the Liebig's Extract of Meat Company as a factory and warehouse. Liebig's commissioned Albert Moore to rebuild the factory in art deco style, transforming the central chimney into a streamlined tower. Liebig's most famous product was the OXO beef stock cube and they envisaged a large external sign. However, with riverside advertising banned Moore cleverly incorporated vertically angled glazing into the tower which, when illuminated, spelt OXO.

Following acquisition by meat company Vestey, Liebig's vacated the site and the building lay empty. Plans by architect Richard Rogers for the Coin Street area in the 1970s and 1980s including demolition of the Oxo Tower were a catalyst for the Coin Street Action Group (CSAG) (see Entry 23) to prevent redevelopment and retain the building for local housing and small businesses. Eventually, in 1984, the GLC purchased the site for £2.7 million, reselling it to the Coin Street Community Builders (CSCB) for £750,000. In 1988, CSCB renovations incorporated essential repairs, the opening up of the arcaded riverside walkway and demolition of buildings, allowing light into new living and work spaces in the refurbished factory. Public access to the courtyard was granted and together with Gabriel's Wharf the area began its renaissance.

This growing popularity generated further development plans and the 1990s witnessed the CSCB working with architects Lifschutz Davidson on a £20 million project with a

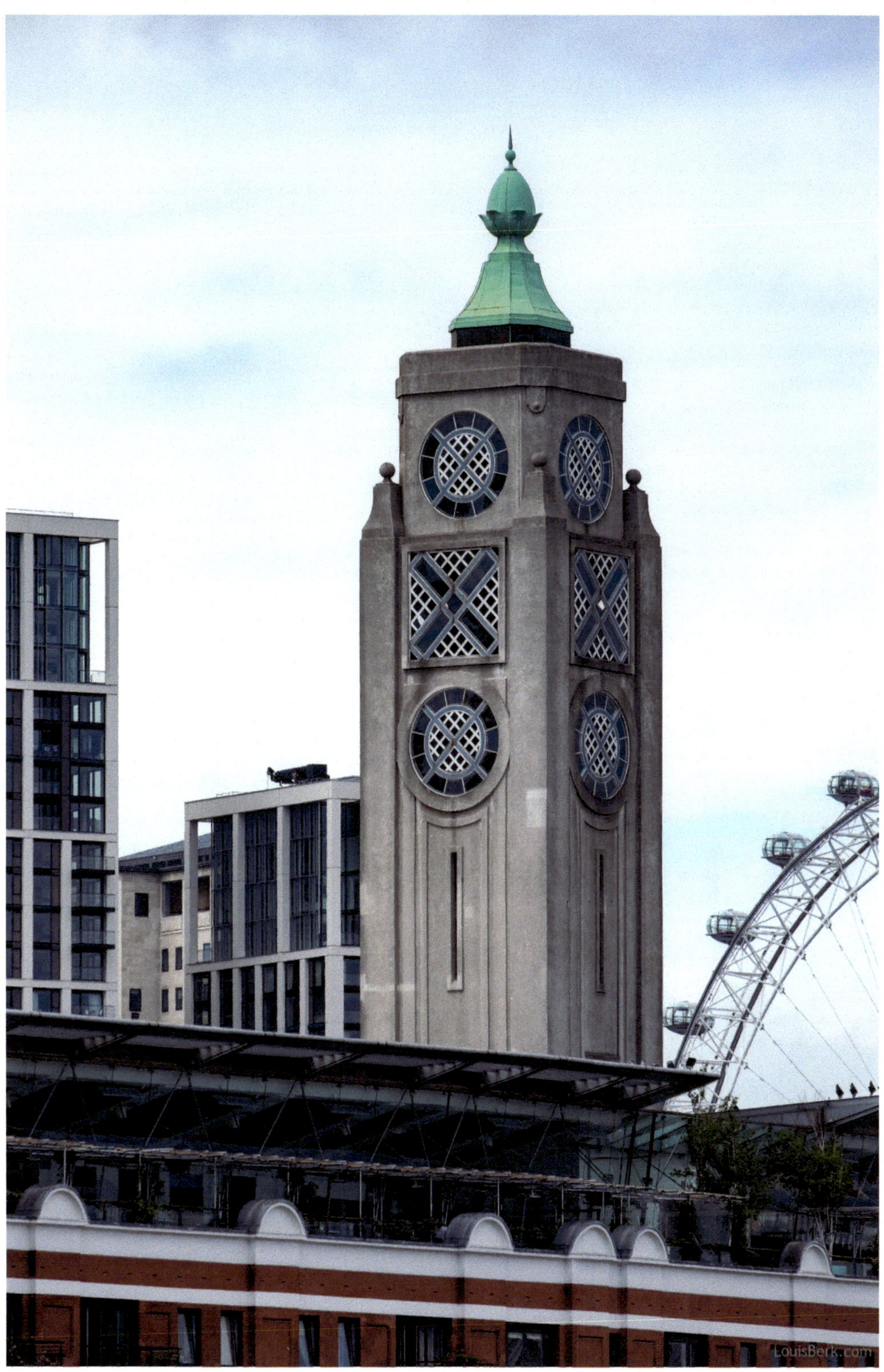

OXO building tower.

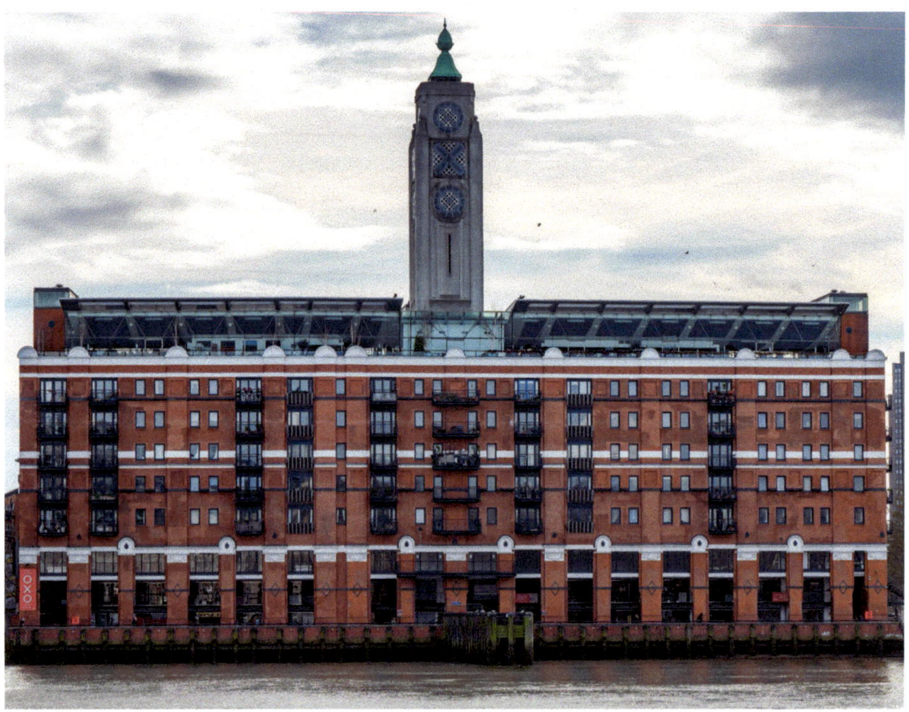

The OXO building.

social housing co-operative of seventy-eight flats, design studios, retail outlets, galleries for designer-makers and an eighth-floor restaurant run by upmarket department store Harvey Nichols. Opening in 1996, The Oxo Tower eatery was an immediate success and remains a destination restaurant nearly thirty years later.

Address: Bargehouse Street, SE1 9PH
Built: 1928/29 – A. W. Moore; 1995 – Lifschutz Davidson
Public Access: Yes
Tube/Rail: Blackfriars, Southwark
Website: coinstreet.org/oxotowerwharf; harveynichols.com/restaurant/the-oxo-tower

25. South Bank Tower

On the corner of Hatfields and Upper Ground is a soaring 151-metre-tall tower. Opened in 1972 as Kings Reach Tower, it stands opposite a point on the north bank of the Thames renamed to honour King George V in his 1935 jubilee year. Since renamed South Bank Tower, its existing height was elevated after much planning and public debate from the original thirty-one-storey, 130-metre-tall building to its present height by adding another ten floors.

Resonant of the mid-1970s Tower 42 in The City, both buildings were designed by Richard Seifert. Two circular halves with stepped extensions are attached to a central elevator and services shaft which gives the impression of a backbone. At the time of construction all-

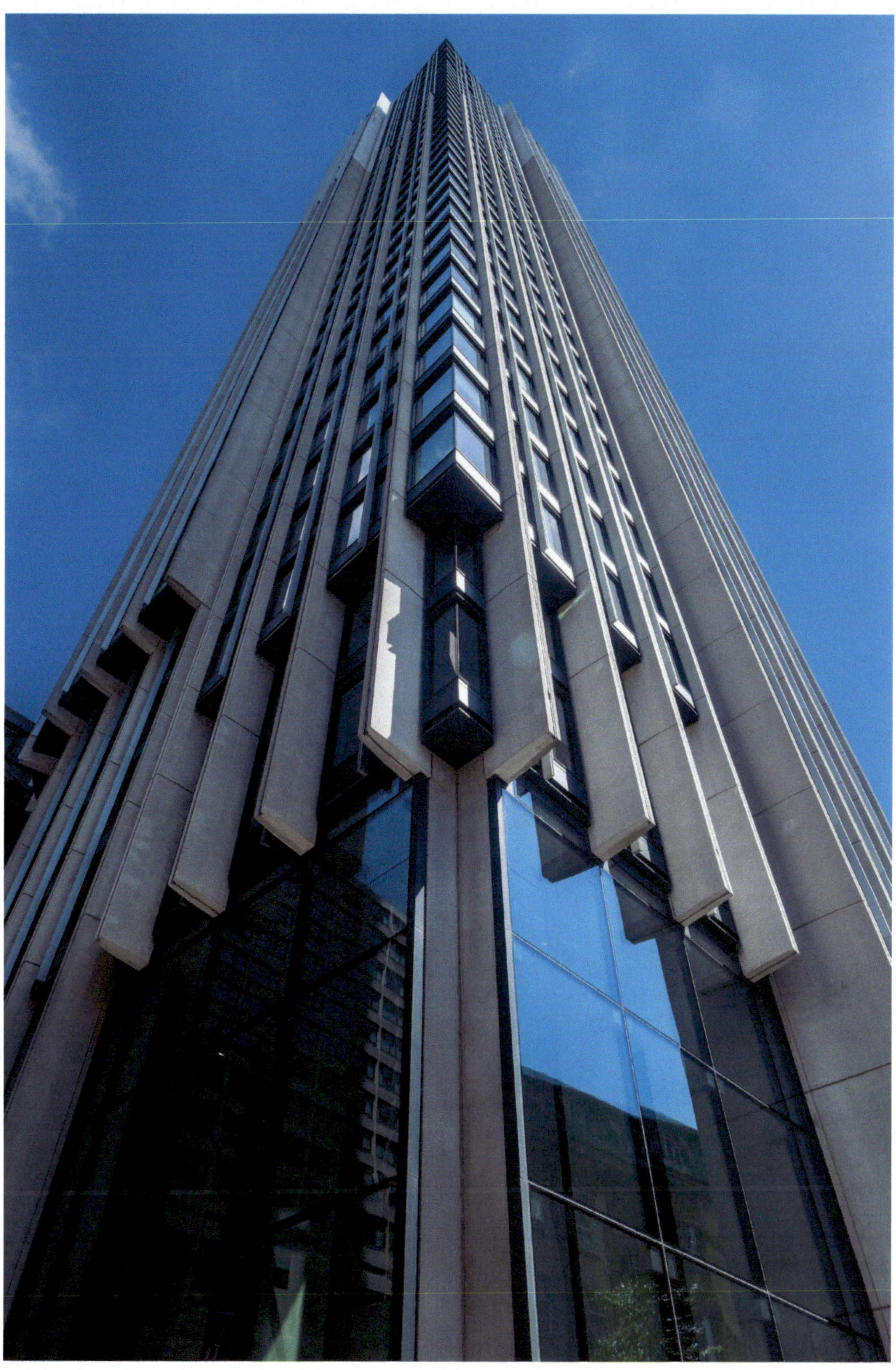

South Bank Tower.

glass exteriors (such as One Blackfriars and The Shard – see Entries 27 and 43) were not yet available, and thin lattices run up the length of the tower to which windows are attached.

IPC Media occupied the building from its completion in 1972 until 2007. One of Europe's biggest publishing companies, it featured the tower in its popular weekly science-fiction comic *2000AD*. An 'alien' editor called Tharg introduced each publication and the tower was referred to as his 'nerve centre'.

Before IPC Media vacated, planning permission was underway to refurbish and raise the height of the tower with the central core reduced in width increasing the area of each floor. Work was completed in 2017.

South Bank Tower has since been converted to apartments offering luxury concierge accommodation with facilities including a gym, spa, cinema room and rooftop gardens.

Address: No. 55 Upper Ground, SE1 9EY
Built: 1972 – Richard Seifert; Renovated 2017
Public Access: No
Tube/Rail: Blackfriars, Southwark, Waterloo

26. Sea Containers London

Situated just west of Blackfriars Bridge, Sea Containers London is one of the area's best-known buildings despite only having been built in 1974 during the early renaissance of

Sea Containers London.

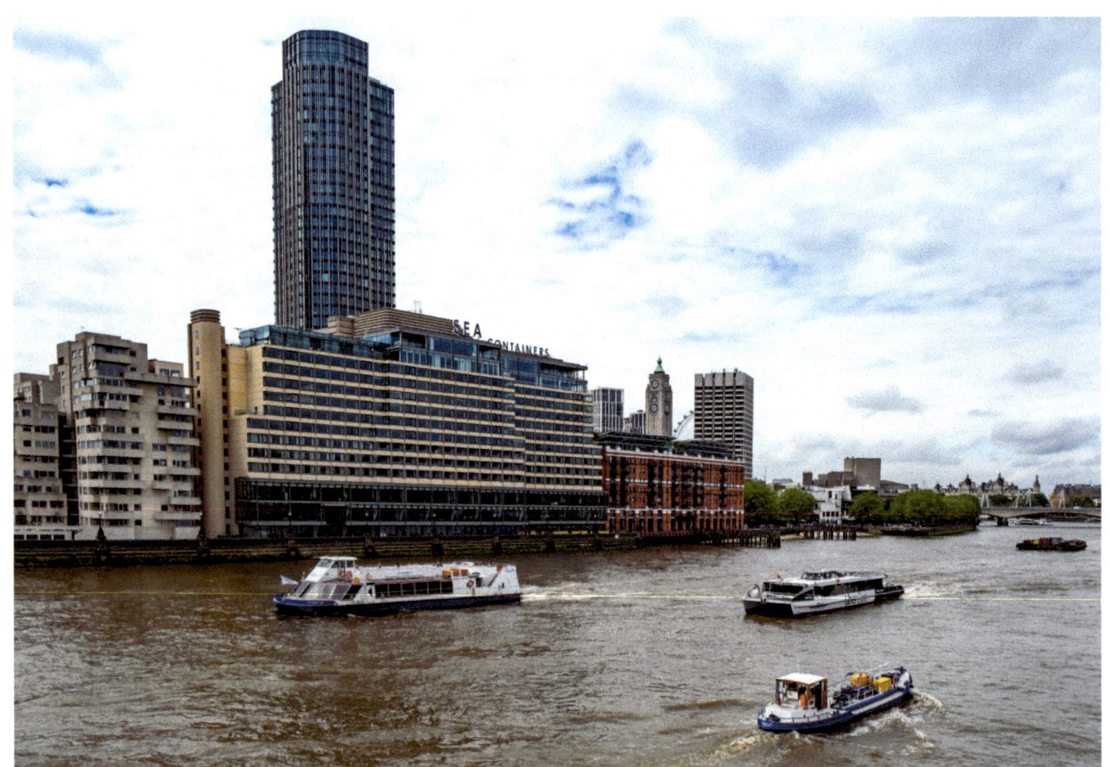

the riverside, at that time fronted by outdated and redundant warehouses. Originally planned as a luxury hotel and designed by Warren Platner Associates, it opened in 1978 as Sea Containers House, offices for a container shipping and transportation business with the same name. The company, founded in 1965, later expanded into hotels, railways, ferries and fruit farming. Sea Containers filed for bankruptcy in 2006, with the building subsequently acquired by an asset management company.

The building was later refurbished by TP Bennett, who added two storeys, removed the golden balls from the skyline, opened up the interior and introduced brand new signage to the riverside. The car park and maintenance yard were filled with a new office block and the Mondrian group of hotels leased the southern block as their first UK hotel in 2014. In 2019 the hotel became independent and was renamed Sea Containers London Hotel, echoing the site's original owners.

WPP, the global advertising, branding and media company, is currently based here but at the time of writing is planning relocation to the former FT site (see Entry 31).

Address: No. 20 Upper Ground, SE1 9PD
Built: 1978 – Warren Platner Associates; Refurbishment 2011/14 – T. P. Bennett
Public Access: Yes
Tube/Rail: Blackfriars, Southwark
Website: seacontainerslondon.com

27. One Blackfriars

The distinctive One Blackfriars is a landmark apartment block at the southern end of the road and rail bridges at Blackfriars. Built on an area of land cleared after Sainsbury's headquarters moved to Holborn, the tower is 163 metres tall with fifty-two storeys. At ground level there are two small additional buildings and a piazza. Architect Ian Simpson claims he was inspired to create its curved and asymmetric shape by the iconic Lansetti glass vase by Finnish artist Timo Tapani Sarpaneva. The design has no straight lines providing a fluid shape and reflective glass allows the building to change colour during the day.

The developers were given planning permission in 2007 but significant objections from LB Southwark, English Heritage and local residents resulted in additional amenities included such as local affordable housing. The original developers went bankrupt and new owners, Berkeley Group's St George subsidiary, broke ground in 2013, completing the building in 2018. When marketing commenced the smallest flat was offered at just over £1 million, with the largest, the Kensington Suite on the 43rd floor, commanding an asking price of £23 million.

The design has led to many nicknames in addition to 'The Vase', on which it is based, including 'The Boomerang', 'The Pregnant Woman', 'The Cyst' and 'The Tummy'.

Address: Nos 1/16 Blackfriars Road, SE1 9GD
Built: 2013/18 – Simpsonhaugh and Partners
Public Access: No
Tube/Rail: Blackfriars, Southwark

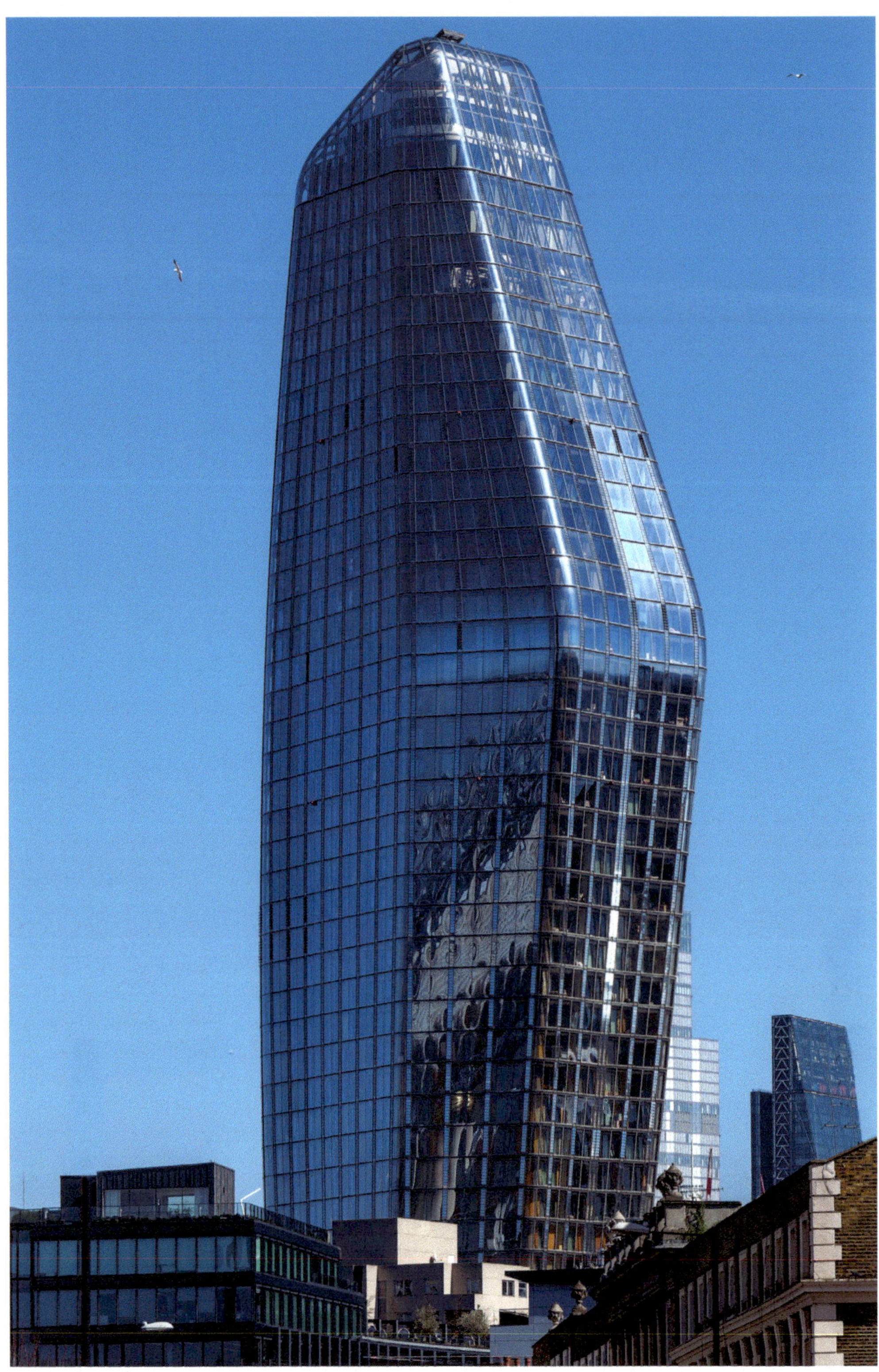

One Blackfriars.

28. Hopton's Almshouses

No greater contrast is likely seen along the south bank than between the vast bulk of the Neo Bankside high-rise apartment blocks and the 1740s Hopton's Almshouses.

Built by livery companies, philanthropists and various charities, they provided accommodation, typically for impoverished retirees. Originally found throughout London and outlying villages, as the population rose the sites became more valuable. Many charities sold their properties to developers and rebuilt them in the growing suburbs so few examples survive in central London, making Hopton's Almshouses particularly notable.

Almshouses are easily recognisable. The homes are usually small, just one storey high, sometimes two. Typically built around a courtyard, there is often a chapel too. Residents were usually given an annual stipend, coal and blankets, depending on the charity's regulations.

Charles Hopton, a wealthy merchant and member of the Fishmongers' Company, died in 1731 making provision for almshouses housing twenty-six unmarried 'poor decayed men' of the local parish of Christ Church, Southwark. Opened in 1752, the site was considered 'the cheapest, best and most convenient piece of ground that could be had for the building'. Each resident was allocated around £10 and an annual chaldron of coal. Early residents included watermen and fishermen reflecting local occupations. Two more almshouses were added in 1825 and gas lighting was introduced in 1830. 1835 improvements included York stone paving and new front gates and railings.

Hopton's Almshouses overshadowed by Neo Bankside.

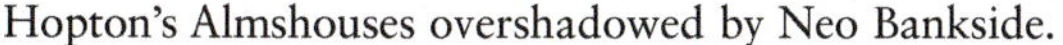

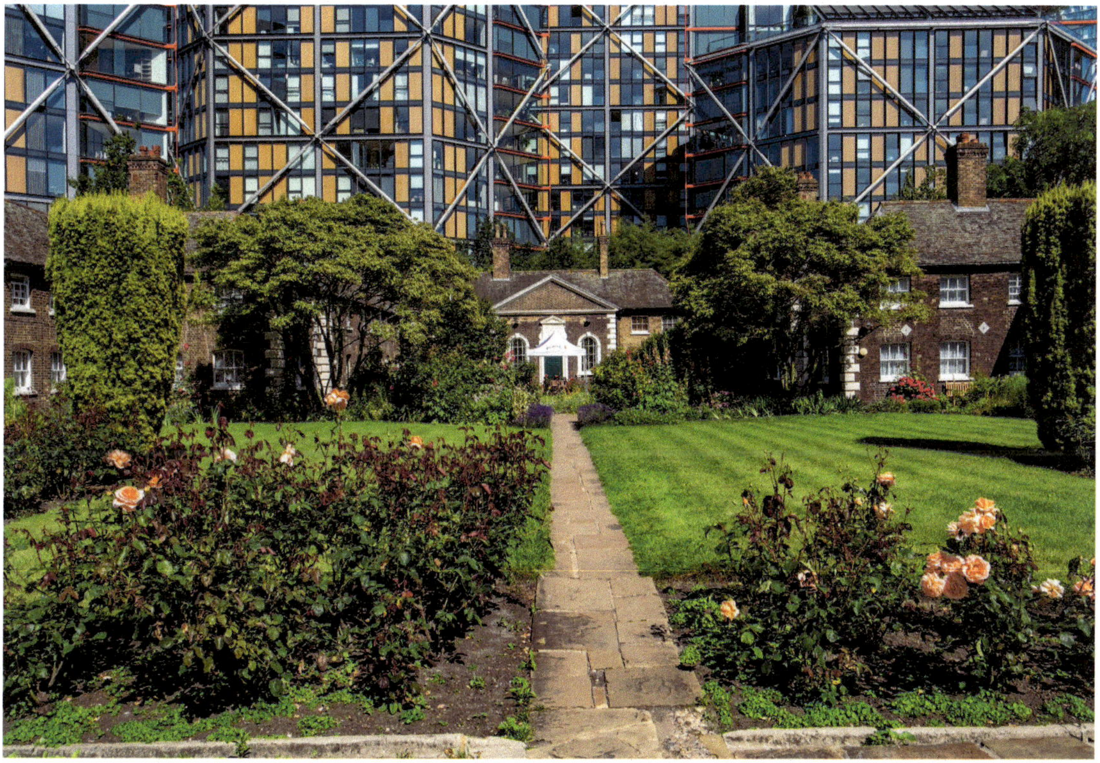

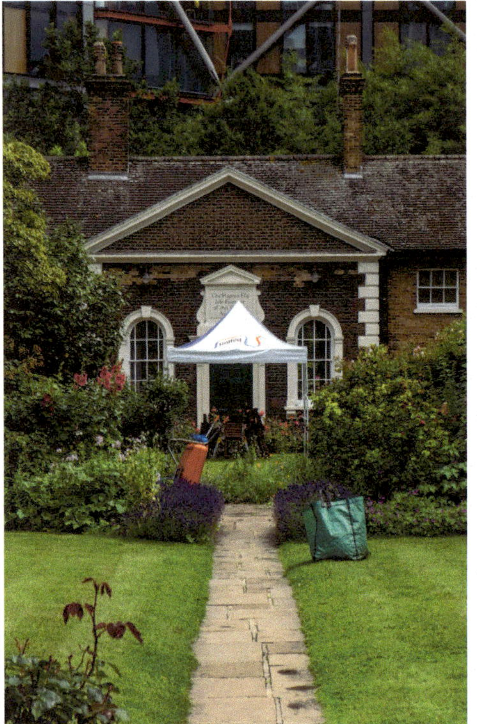

Central entrance to the almshouses.

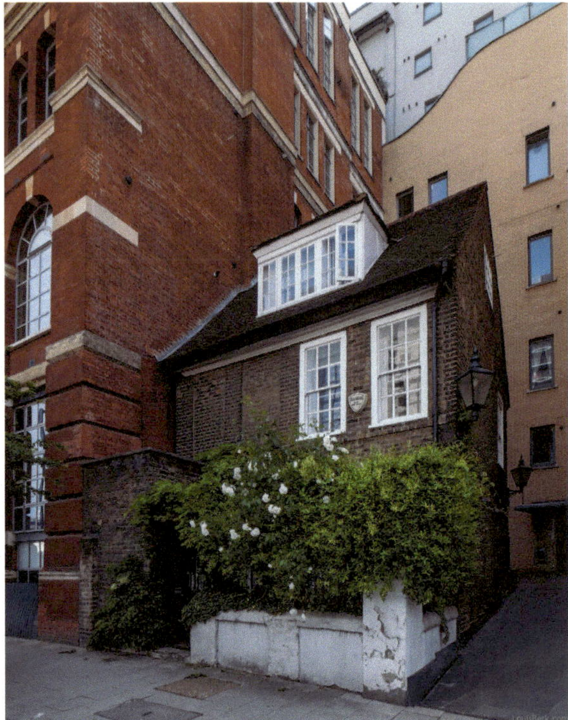

Surviving house on Hopton Street.

Behind the almshouses were twenty-eight small garden plots and a drying area and today the homes look out onto two small well maintained gardens. Hidden from public view are additional private and communal gardens. Following Blitz damage, rebuilding restored full occupancy by 1962.

Management passed to the Anchor Trust and following modernisation reducing the number of homes to twenty, the accommodation reopened in 1988. In 2011 the United St Saviour's Charity took ownership. The John Fry Room, a communal activity and meeting space, commemorates the generosity of the proprietor of Fry's Metal Foundry on Holland Street, where Neo Bankside stands today.

Address: Nos 10/11 Hopton Street, SE1 9JJ
Built: 1745/49 – Thomas Ellis, William Cooley
Listed Status: Grade II*
Public Access: No
Tube/Rail: Blackfriars, Southwark

29. Tate Modern

Tate Modern, dominating the view across the river from St. Paul's Cathedral, opened in 2000 as a millennium project solving two conundrums: how to accommodate The Tate Gallery's growing modern art collection and repurpose a disused power station which ceased operations in 1981.

The power station, constructed in two stages between 1947 and 1963 and designed by Giles Gilbert Scott, the architect of Battersea Power Station further west, is instantly recognisable by its single chimney, 99 metres high, intentionally shorter than the dome and cross of St. Paul's Cathedral across the river. The chimney rises from a vast structure of 4.2 million London stock bricks and containing a turbine hall 35 metres high and 152 metres long. After closing in 1981 just an adjoining switch house remained in use as an electricity sub-station.

By the early 1990s a creative community on Bankside was emerging and in 1992 it was decided to split the Tate into two sites, with the original Tate Gallery showcasing British art pre-1900 and renamed Tate Britain, and European modern art post-1900 moving to a new gallery, Tate Modern. In 1994 Bankside Power Station was selected as the site and in 1995 Herzog and de Meuron of Switzerland were appointed as architects. The character of the original building was retained with a two-storey light box added to the roof providing

Tate Modern from Millennium Bridge.

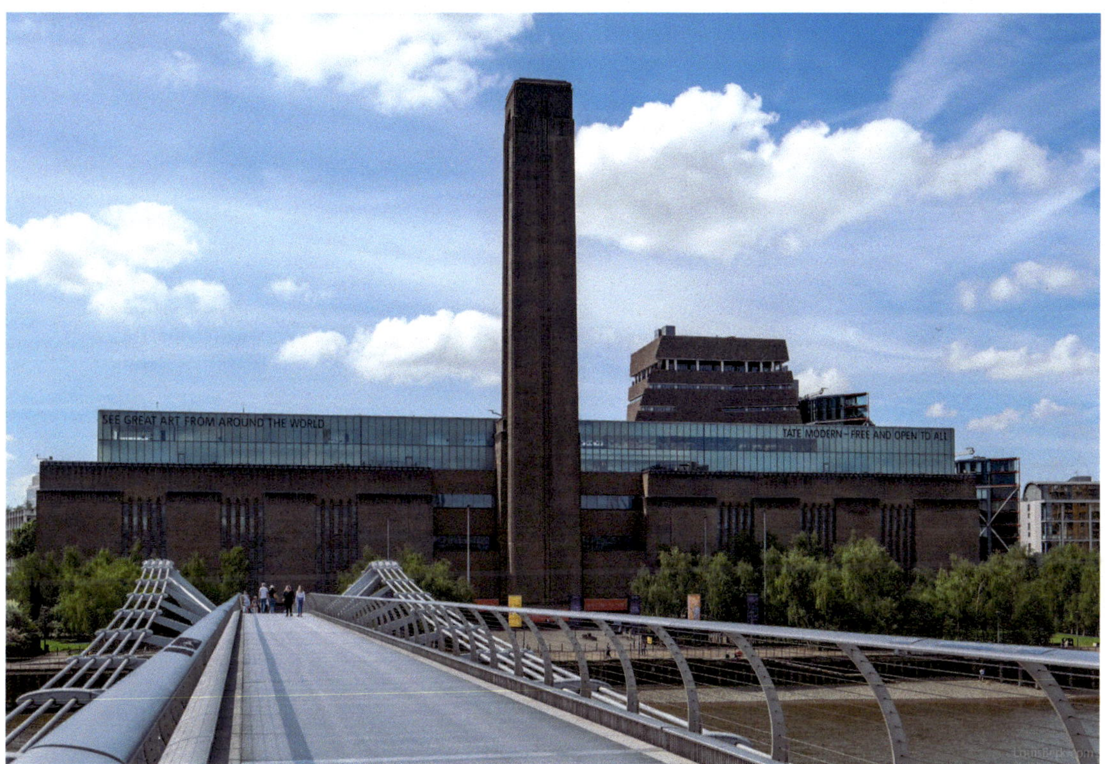

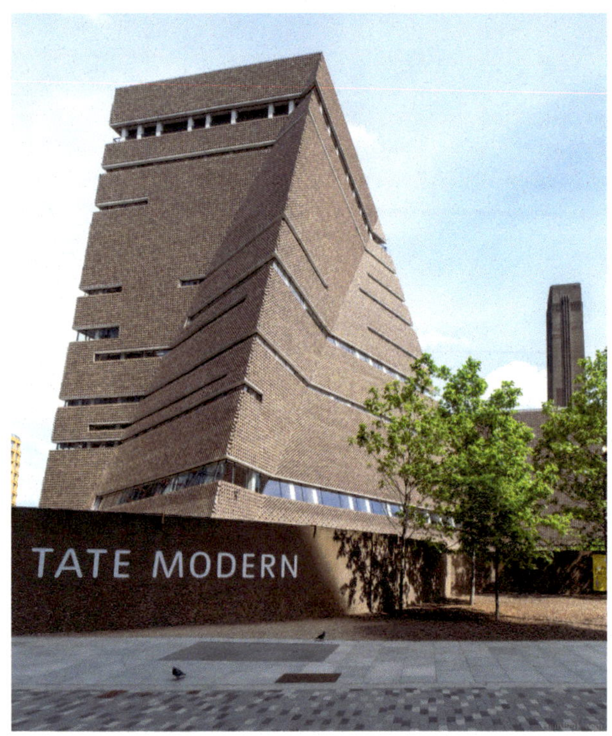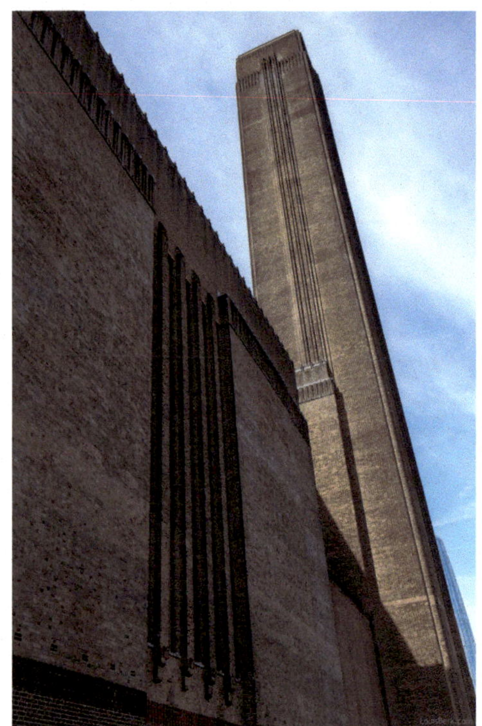

Above left: Blavatnik Building, Tate Modern.

Above right: Imposing brick façade of the power station.

café facilities, natural light and views across to St Paul's and beyond. The Turbine Hall, accessed by a ramp, provided a dramatic setting for regularly changing large-scale installations commissioned from eminent contemporary artists including Anish Kapoor and Rachel Whiteread. Within a year Tate Modern had welcomed 5 million visitors. The art collection is regularly re-hung, enabling it to be viewed and considered in different ways.

Tate Modern has continued to expand. The Boiler House within the power station has been converted into installation spaces and, behind the gallery, the Blavatnik Building opened in 2016. Originally called The Switch House, reflecting its original use, the name now honours key donor Len Blavatnik. The red brickwork in a lattice style complements the red brick of the original building.

Address: Bankside, SE1 9TG
Built: 1947/1963 – Giles Gilbert Scott; 1995/2000 – Herzog and de Meuron
Public Access: Yes, free but exhibitions are charged
Tube: Southwark
Website: tate.org.uk

30. Shakespeare's Globe

The first thatched building to be erected in London since the Great Fire of 1666 is a replica of the Globe Theatre. First built on Bankside in 1599 by a consortium including William Shakespeare, the original Globe burnt down in 1613, rebuilt a year later but demolished

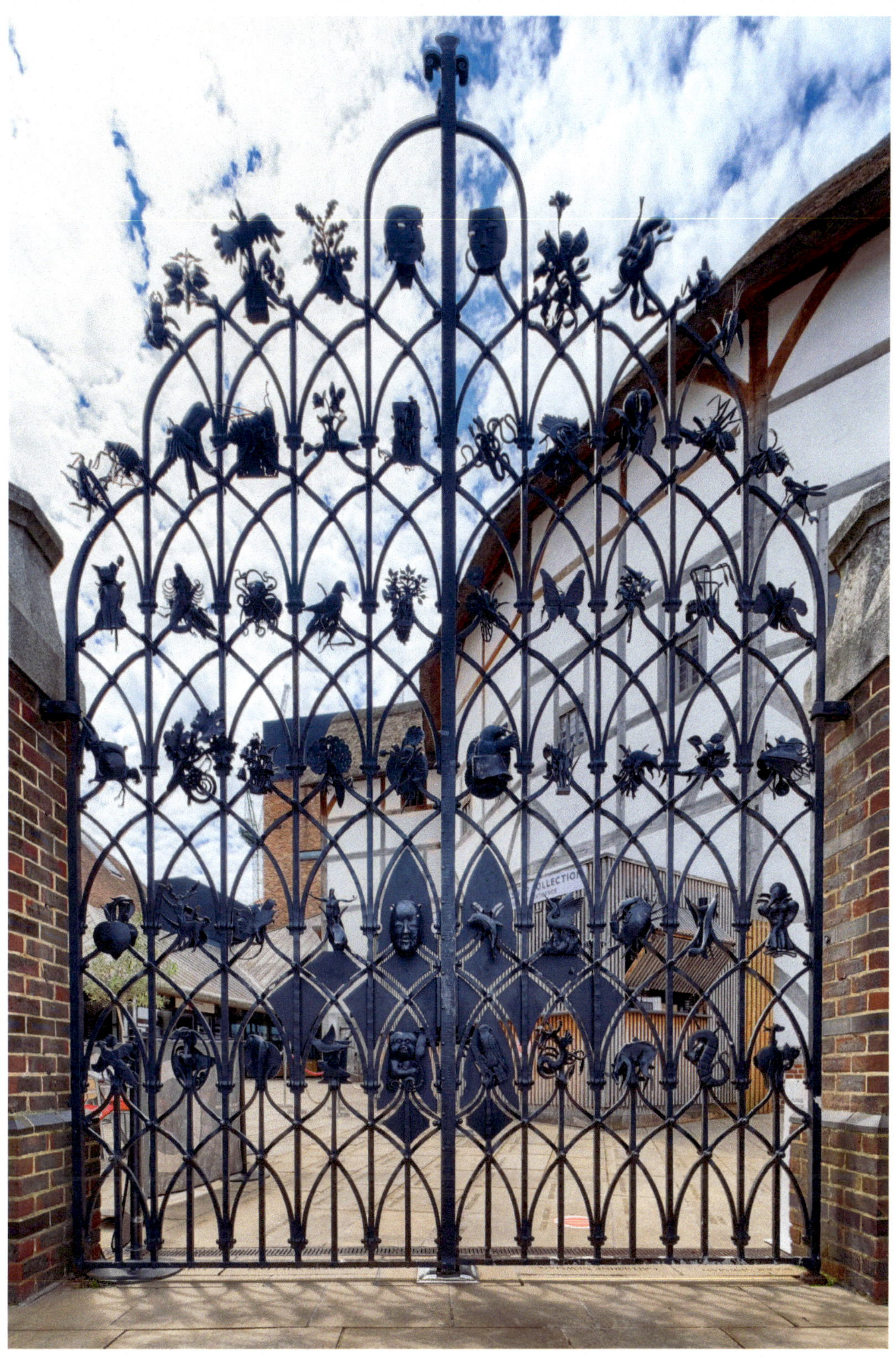

Ironwork gate, Shakespeare's Globe.

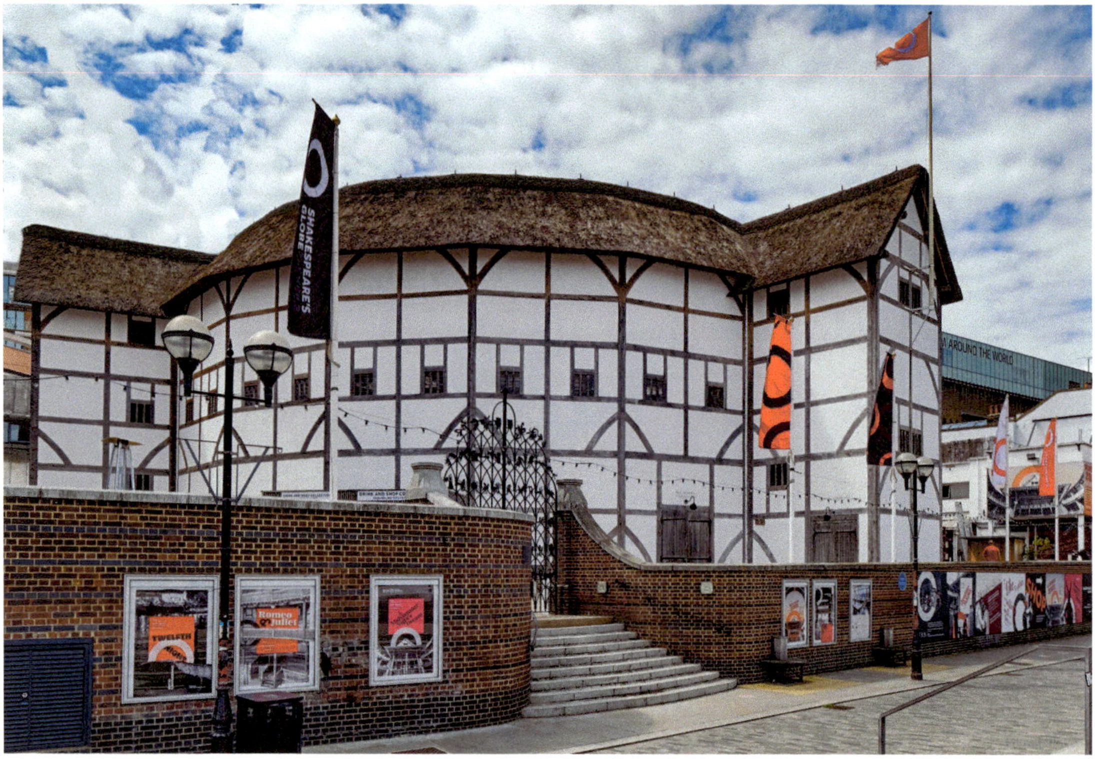

Above: Shakespeare's Globe, Bankside.

Below: Park Street plaque at the location of the original Globe Theatre.

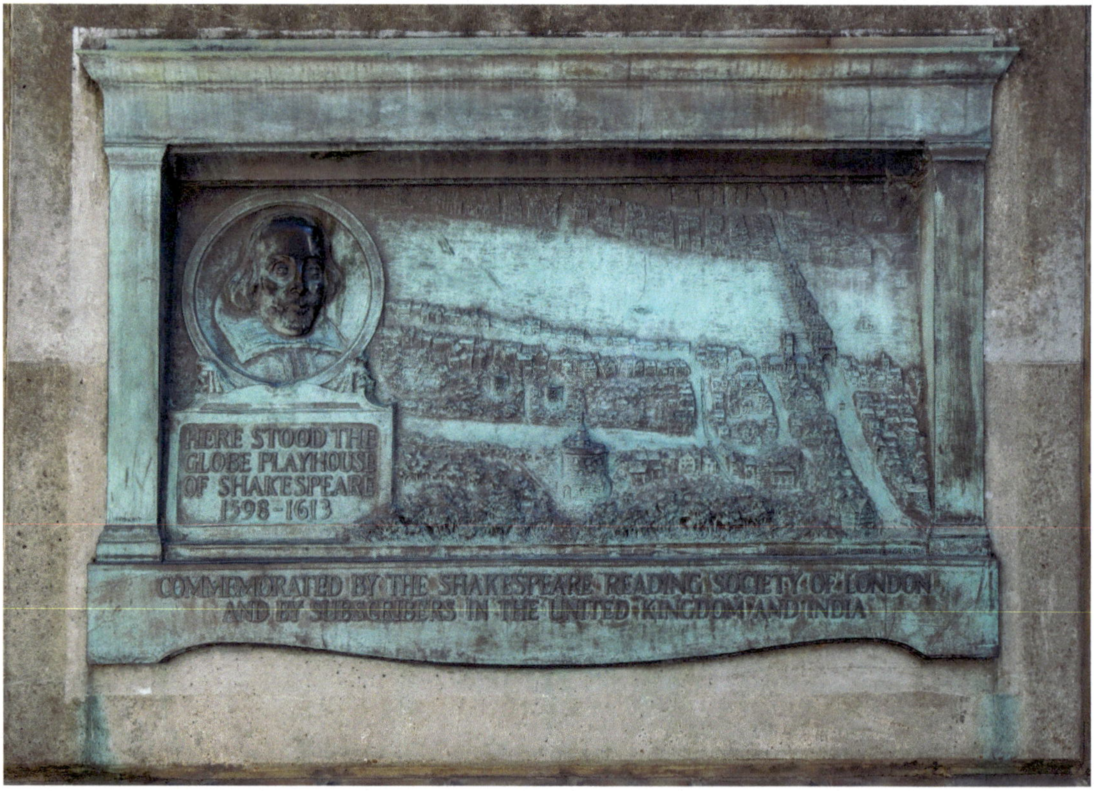

in 1642 by order of the Puritans. Today's theatre, branded as Shakespeare's Globe, was the vision of American actor and director Sam Wanamaker, who established the Globe Playhouse Trust to reconstruct the 'Wooden O', as referenced in Shakespeare's *Henry V*. Wanamaker died in 1993 before the theatre opened in 1997 but a plaque commemorates him on the riverside wall and in 2014 an additional auditorium, the Sam Wanamaker Playhouse, opened. Seating 340, it is reminiscent of a seventeenth-century indoor theatre with wooden panels and galleries.

A pair of wrought-iron gates opens from the riverside. Made by 130 different blacksmiths from twelve different countries, there are over 100 figures of animals, creatures and plants mentioned in Shakespeare's plays. Paving stones seen through the gates name donors who funded the project.

The main public entrance around the corner leads to the foyer and thence to the paved plaza and circular theatre. The stage, protruding into the auditorium, is protected from the weather by a canopy whose painted ceiling resembles a starry heaven. Groundlings, theatregoers with no seats, can gather round three sides of the stage as they did in the 1600s. The timber framework and seating has been made to Elizabethan construction techniques apart from modern safety essentials such as fire prevention sprinklers and strict capacity limits. Eagle-eyed visitors can spot the tiny sprinkler heads peeping out from the thatched roof and instead of the 3,000 spectators of Shakespeare's day, audiences are no more than 1,570. For those not attending a performance, tours and exhibition spaces are part of an extensive educational programme.

A short detour to Park Street leads to the original Globe Theatre site and the memorial plaque that inspired Sam Wanamaker. Now a housing complex, a curved slate marker delineates the footprint of the theatre.

Address: No. 21 New Globe Walk, SE1 9DT
Built: 1997 – Jon Greenfield, Theo Crosby
Public Access: Yes
Tube/Rail: London Bridge, Southwark
Website: shakespearesglobe.com

31. One Southwark Bridge Road

Between 1989 and 2019, the seven-storey building nestling alongside the southern approach to Southwark Bridge was the purpose-built HQ for international business newspaper the Financial Times (FT). Several critics were harsh, one calling it 'a tinted glass box with a cheap-looking blue metal roof', although others considered it distinguished and the large letters FT stood out against pink tinted glazing, a nod to the FT's famous pink paper. Designed for a specific occupier, the interior was conducive to writing within the deadline-oriented atmosphere of a newspaper. Its position on the south bank of the Thames made it in some ways a City outsider while being very much key to the City.

Arriving in 1989, the FT witnessed the rapid transformation to the neighbourhood but in 2019 returned to its original City HQ, Bracken House on Cannon Street, and this riverside

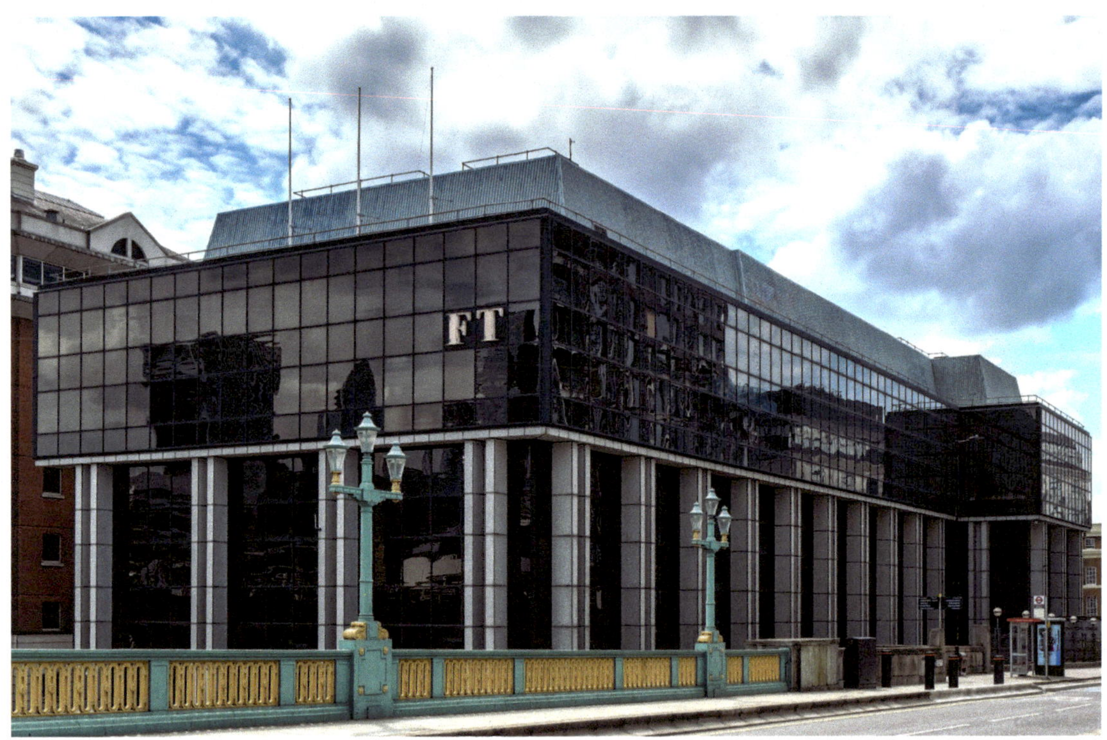

One Southwark Bridge Road, the FT building (pre-redevelopment).

building will become the HQ for WPP, a global advertising company. The £90 million project includes state-of-the-art office provision, additional access points, affordable workspace, public spaces and a new north-south public walkway between Park Street and the Thames, while the railway arches will be repurposed. Redevelopment commenced during the publication of this book.

Address: One Southwark Bridge Road, SE1 9HL
Built: 1987 – T. P. Bennett; Redevelopment 2020s – BDG
Public Access: No
Tube/Rail: Blackfriars, Southwark

32. The Anchor Public House

The Anchor, with its bright red window frames and floral window displays, is one of London's busiest and prettiest riverside pubs. Constructed between 1770 and 1775 and rebuilt in the early nineteenth century, the site had previously been the 'tap room' for the nearby Anchor Brewery on Park Street. The name is believed to date back to 1665 as brewery owner Josiah Childs had close ties with the navy. In the 1980s the brewery buildings were demolished and replaced by housing with its perimeter walls holding a series of commemorative plaques.

It was at the heart of what was the notoriously noisy and very likely pungent entertainment and industrial area of Bankside, with breweries, brothels (see Entry 34),

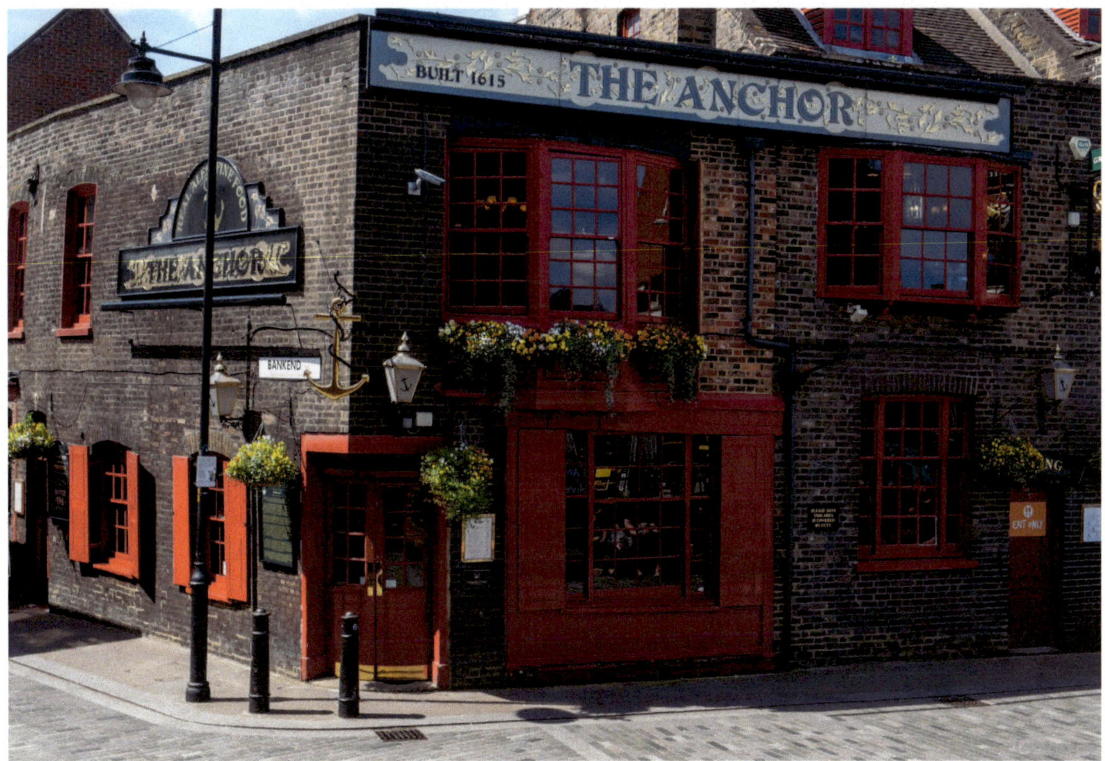

The Anchor public house.

theatres and bear-baiting gardens. Stories link to Samuel Pepys, smuggling and contraband hidden behind ceiling beams and in secret compartments scattered around the tavern. The Anchor has been used several times as a film location including *Mission Impossible* with Tom Cruise in 1996.

The pub is officially part of the neighbouring Premier Inn with its east wall on Bank End, indicating perhaps the official easterly boundary of Bankside.

Address: No. 34 Park Street, SE1 9EF
Built: 1770s; Refurbished 2008
Public Access: Yes
Tube/Rail: London Bridge, Southwark
Website: greeneking-pubs.co.uk

33. The Clink

A skeleton hanging in an iron gibbet above the street and the instruction on the door 'Ring (bell) for jailer' prepares visitors for what awaits them as they enter The Clink.

Housed in the basement of a Victorian warehouse, this compact visitor attraction brings to life the story of one of London's most famous prisons, from which, allegedly, the phrase to be 'in the Clink' originates, from the sound of the chains around prisoners' feet.

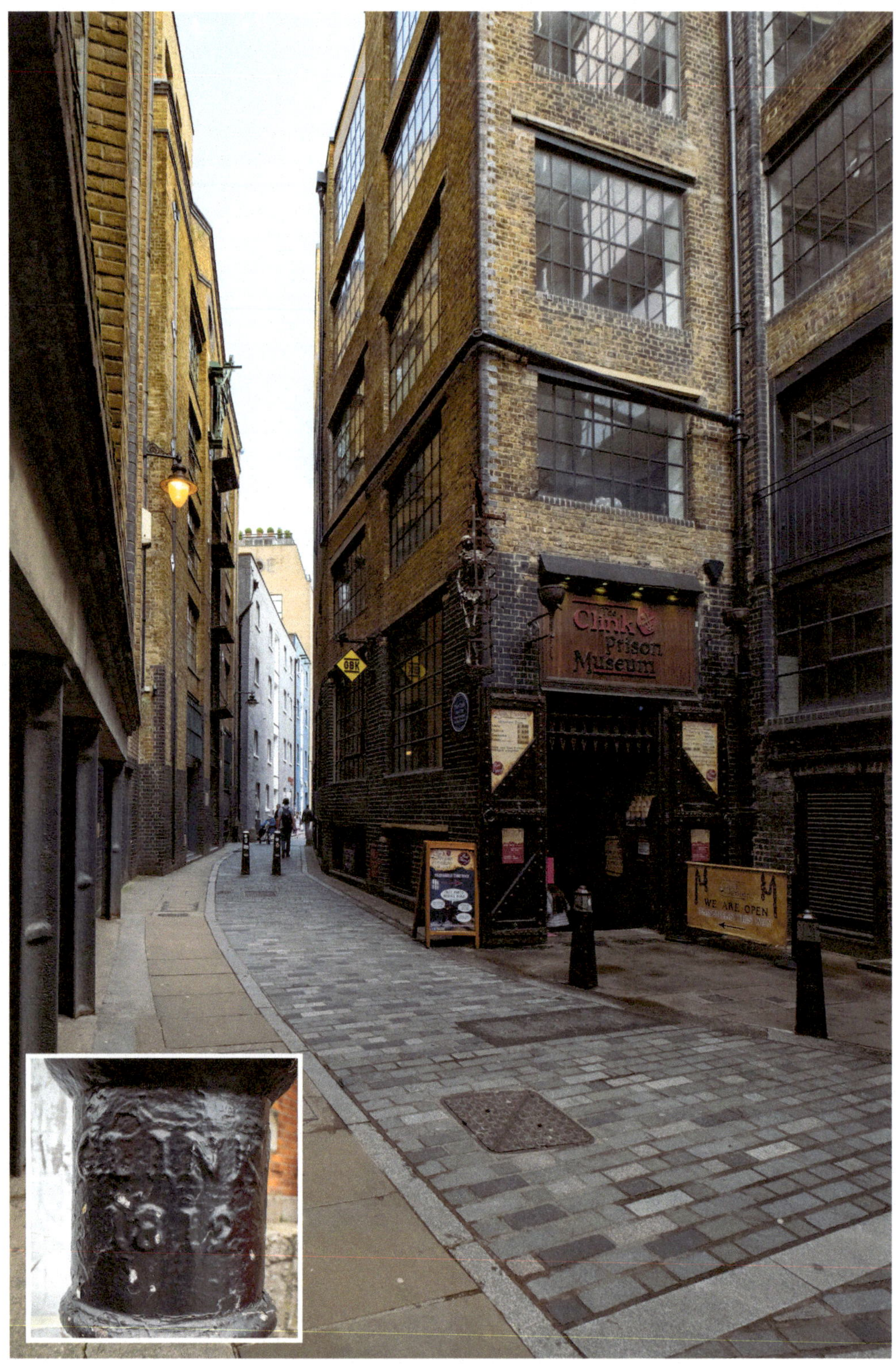

Clink Street. *Insert*: Clink 1812 bollards.

The prison is thought to have originated in the mid-twelfth century as small cells, one for men and one for women, built within Winchester Palace (see Entry 34). Over time it gradually enlarged to a full-sized prison housing mostly petty criminals, vagrants, prostitutes and brothel keepers but also political and religious victims. Damaged during the 1381 Peasants' Revolt and a 1450 rebellion, it was rebuilt as a two-storey prison for men but it could not survive the 1780 Gordon Riots where Protestants, angry with concessions granted to Catholics, razed the building to the ground, releasing the prisoners. Almost nothing remains except the name of the street and part of a wall, now within the museum.

As visitors descend the staircase the atmosphere changes dramatically to a labyrinth of dark damp rooms with sounds of groans and wails evoking the lives of those previously jailed here. Exhibits tell the story of prisoners, torture instruments and gruesome details of day-to-day life, within the wider context of riverside life between the twelfth and eighteenth centuries.

Address: No. 1 Clink Street, SE1 9DG
Built: 1800s (the warehouse)
Public Access: Yes. Advised for ages seven years and above
Tube/Rail: London Bridge, Southwark
Website: clink.co.uk

34. Winchester Palace

The remains of the Great Hall of Winchester Palace emerge amidst the cafés and souvenir shops along Clink Street. One of the largest and most important buildings of medieval London, Winchester Palace was built in the twelfth century by King Stephen's brother, Bishop Henry de Blois, who required luxury accommodation for visiting bishops. Bishops' palaces, once numbering around 150 around the UK, were large estates incorporating dining, worship and lodging facilities for bishops and their servants.

The size of the Great Hall, gauged by surviving tracery of the west gable's rose window, indicates a space 24 metres long, 11 metres wide and 13 metres high, with access to kitchens and a buttery and crypt below for storing beer and wine. Direct access to the Thames allowed for deliveries via three wharves allocated to the bishop. The 6-acre estate included a brewhouse, stables, a slaughterhouse, tennis courts and a bowling alley. It was a place for fun and pleasure, including royal wedding feasts and numerous brothels, known as 'stews'. Local prostitutes were nicknamed Winchester Geese as their long white gloves, indicating allegiance to the bishop, were reminiscent of the long necks of geese. Such activity ended in 1545 with the Dissolution of the Monasteries. The estate also included a prison, known as The Clink (see Entry 33).

The last resident bishop died in 1626 and the buildings were repurposed as warehouses and homes. A fire in 1814 uncovered the remains of the medieval palace but commercial expediency necessitated swift rebuilding, incorporating the newly discovered ruins. The area remained cut off from public view and access until the neighbourhood's 1980s regeneration, when, with access to the riverside, Clink Street once again became a busy thoroughfare.

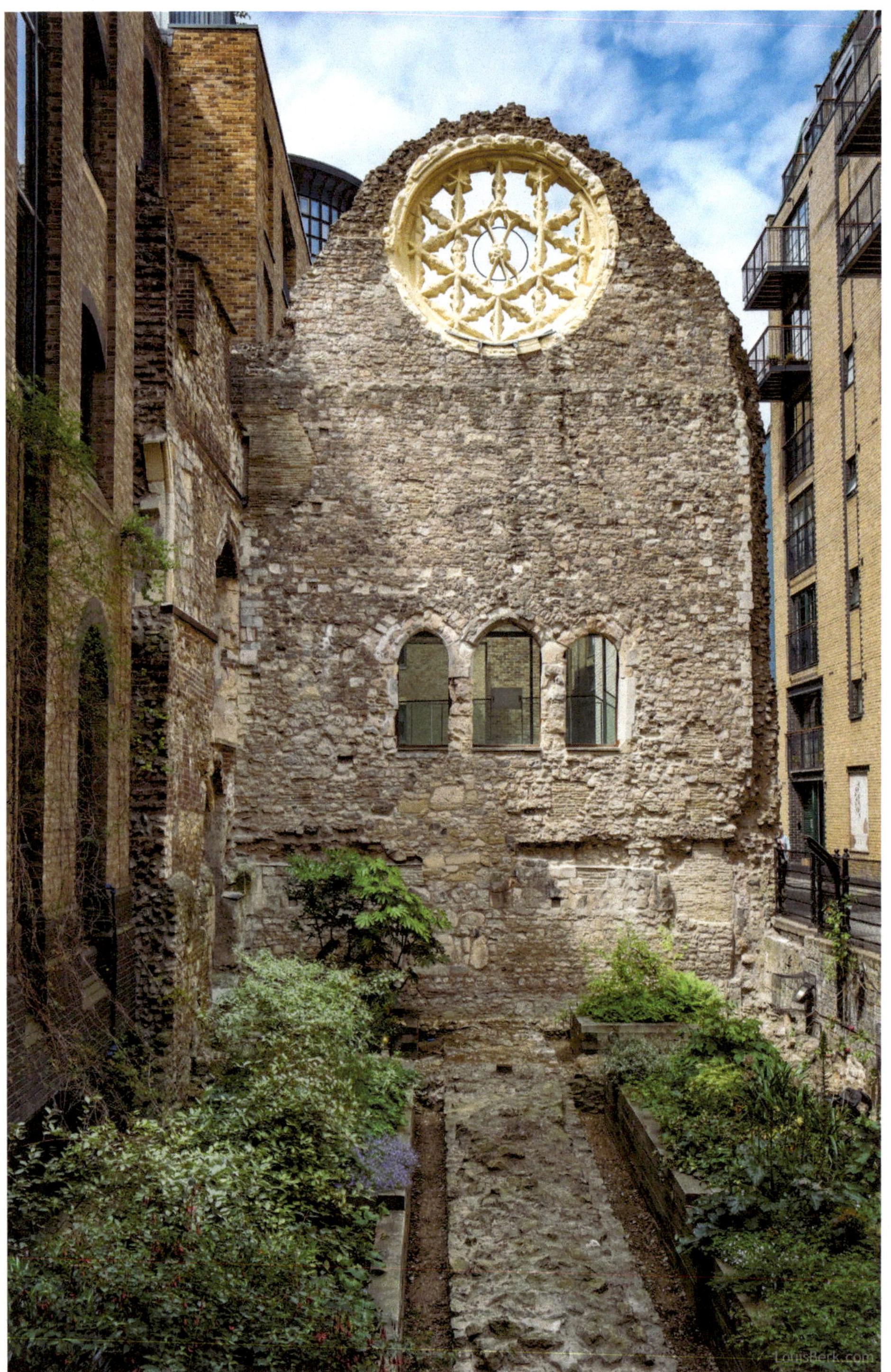

Bishop of Winchester's Palace.

Since 2014 a medieval style garden within the footprint of the Great Hall has been planted by Bankside Open Spaces Trust, bringing a burst of green to an otherwise monochrome street.

Address: Clink Street, SE1 9DG
Built: 1151/61
Listed Status: Grade II*
Public Access: Yes
Tube/Rail: London Bridge, Southwark

35. Pickfords Wharf

Next to the *Golden Hinde* (see Entry 36) is one of the few remaining dockland buildings – Pickfords Wharf. Built in 1864 as Phoenix Wharf, the name changed in 1897 when Pickfords acquired the site for granaries and general warehouses. In 1921, Hay's took ownership but retained the name and in 1948 also purchased St Mary Overie wharf, incorporating it into Pickfords. The complex of buildings on both sides of Clink Street, built around and including the remains of Winchester Palace (see Entry 34), were linked by iron walkways with a first-floor level bridge added in 1920. Both wharves made use of the small inlet alongside, St Mary

Pickfords Wharf.

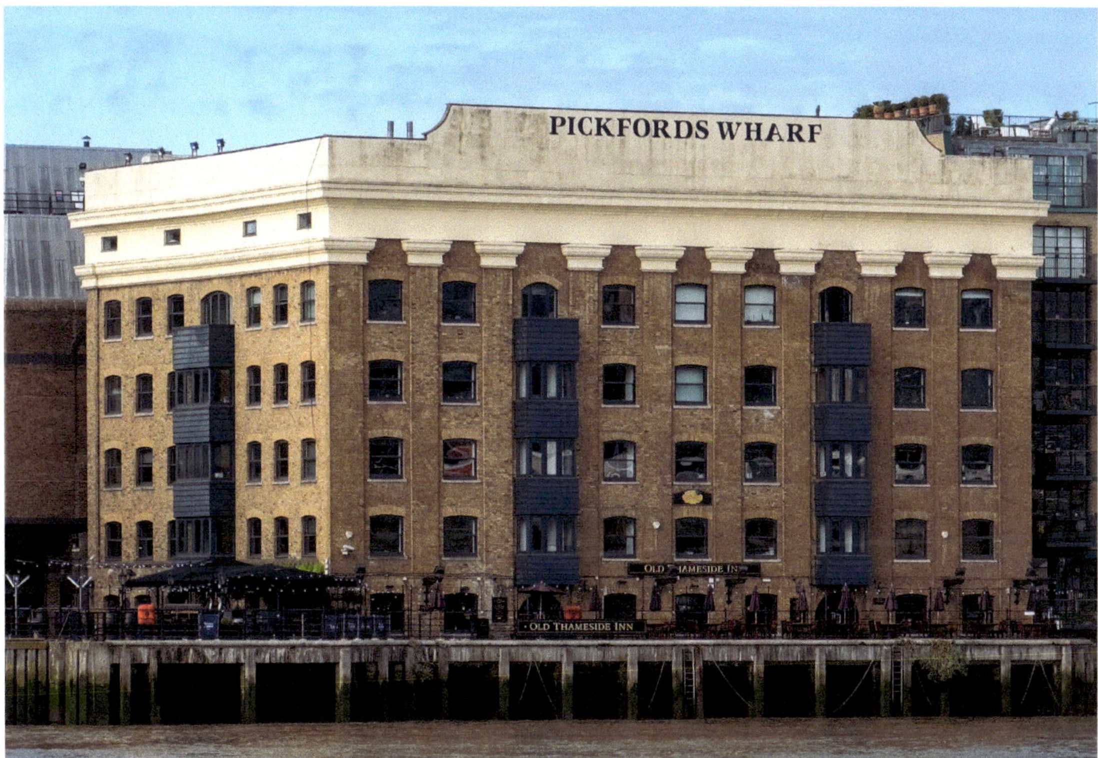

Overie Dock. Goods stored changed through the decades from sugar, flour, apples, oats and potatoes in the late nineteenth century to vegetable fats and India rubber by 1920. By the mid-1960s Pickfords was primarily storing carpets, cardboard boxes and wines and spirits.

Following the 1960s closure of London's docks, the buildings were mainly left to decay before demolition in 1983, along with Rosing's and Stave wharves also owned by Hay's. Only Pickfords A and B warehouses survived. New buildings added in 1983 were designed by architects Michael Twigg Brown (see Entries 40 and 45) to resemble nineteenth-century warehouses. The riverside fascia proclaims Pickfords Wharf but the products within are apartments, offices and a pub, The Old Thameside Inn.

Address: Clink Street, SE1 9DG
Built: 1864; additions and rebuild 1980s
Public Access: Pub only
Tube/Rail: London Bridge

36. *Golden Hinde*

Within the small dry dock of St Mary Overie is a full-sized replica of the *Golden Hinde*, an Elizabethan warship famous for the first circumnavigation of the world between 1577 and 1580. Captained by Francis Drake (later Sir), the original ship disintegrated and was broken up in the late 1600s. This replica is the result of years of painstaking research and craftsmanship. Launched in 1973, it too subsequently circumnavigated the world, eventually travelling over 140,000 miles before being permanently berthed at Southwark in 1996.

The 27-metre-high main mast, sails and figurehead, a head of a gilded female deer (a hind), dominate the site. One of Drake's key patrons was Sir Christopher Hatton and a golden hind featured on his family coat of arms. As recognition of his financial support the ship changed its name from *The Pelican* mid voyage. A Tudor rose and ER represent Queen Elizabeth I, the monarch during Drake's voyages. Below is a large painted golden hind against a blue background and the Hatton family motto in Latin, Cassis Tutissima Virtus ('virtue is the safest helmet'). Below the overhanging deck near the water line is a lion's head to ward off dangerous sea creatures. The flag flown is white with the red cross of St George. The size belies activity within a ship 37 metres long. Found among the five decks are the captain's cabin, sailors' living quarters, food and water storage, small boats, the kitchen galley, the armoury, which doubled as officers' accommodation, workspace for skilled crew such as carpenters and sail makers, the Great Cabin where the officers relaxed and the bilge holding ballast to steady the ship.

Drake's crew would have totalled around eighty, of whom just fifty-six returned in 1580. The twentieth century crew numbered fewer than twenty including the master and cook.

Today's 'crew' welcome visitors on board and recount tales of ship's biscuits, loading cannons and treasures captured from Spanish ships.

Address: St Mary Overie Dock, Cathedral Street, SE1 9DE
Built: 1971/73 – J. Hinks Shipyard
Public Access: Yes; overnight stays available
Tube/Rail: London Bridge
Website: goldenhinde.co.uk

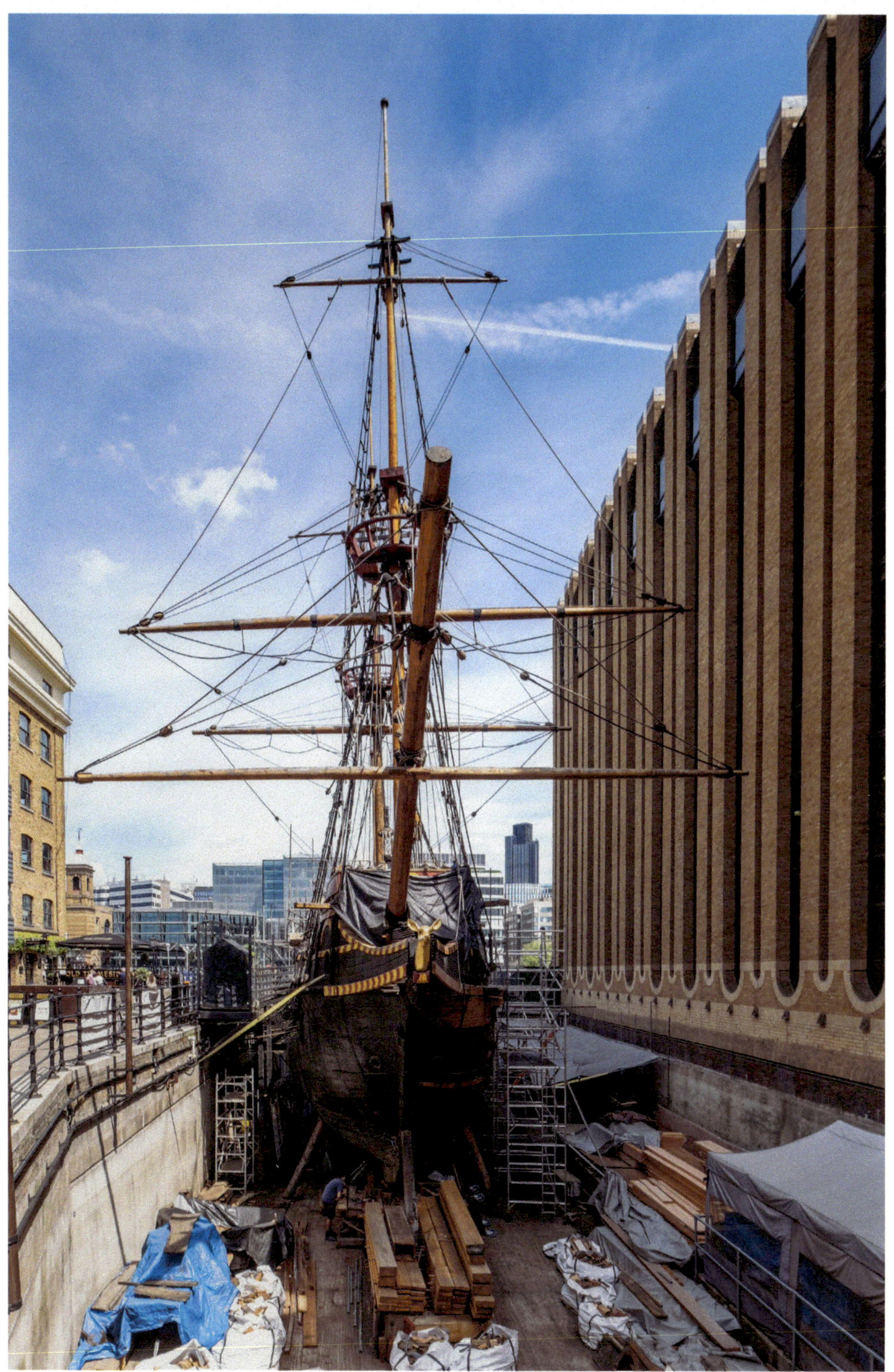

Recreated *Golden Hinde*.

37. Southwark Cathedral

Nestling between London Bridge and Borough Market is the Cathedral and Collegiate Church of St Saviour and St Mary Overie (sometimes written as Overy and meaning 'over the water') known as Southwark Cathedral. The oldest building in Southwark, there has been a church on this site for over 1,000 years, with written records as far back as the 1086 Domesday Book.

Following the 1530s Dissolution of the Monasteries it became the parish church of St Saviour with part of the cloisters and residential quarters granted to the Montagu family, hence Montagu Close alongside. The early sixteenth-century tower was restored in the 1820s and the nave totally reconstructed between 1891/96 by Reginald Blomfield. In 1905 the church was accorded cathedral status for the new Anglican diocese of Southwark, a vast area currently administering to 2.5 million residents. Inside the church are a host of literary associations. John Harvard, founder of Harvard University in the USA, was baptised here in 1607 and a memorial window commemorates the tercentenary of his birth and memorials are also found to Chaucer, John Bunyan, James Burbage of the Globe Theatre (see Entry 30) and the playwright William Shakespeare, whose younger brother Edmund's funeral in 1607 was held here.

For centuries the eastern side was almost entirely hidden from view, except for the tower, until the 1820s when Borough High Street was reconfigured. The north elevation was subsequently concealed by wharves and warehouses built in 1837, but as part of the 1977 Silver Jubilee commemorations these were demolished, creating a new public space with views across the Thames. Extensive refurbishment between 1997 and 2012 by Richard Griffiths cleaned and floodlit the exterior, with a new courtyard providing public access from the Thames walkway. This group of new buildings incorporated income-generating amenities including education rooms, a shop, a café and conference facilities.

Address: London Bridge, SE1 9DA
Built: 1106; rebuilt 1220s; various alterations 1800s; Refurbishment 1891/96 – Reginald Blomfield; Refurbishment 1997/2012 – Richard Griffiths
Listed Status: Grade I
Public Access: Yes
Tube/Rail: London Bridge
Website: cathedral.southwark.anglican.org

Opposite: Southwark Cathedral.

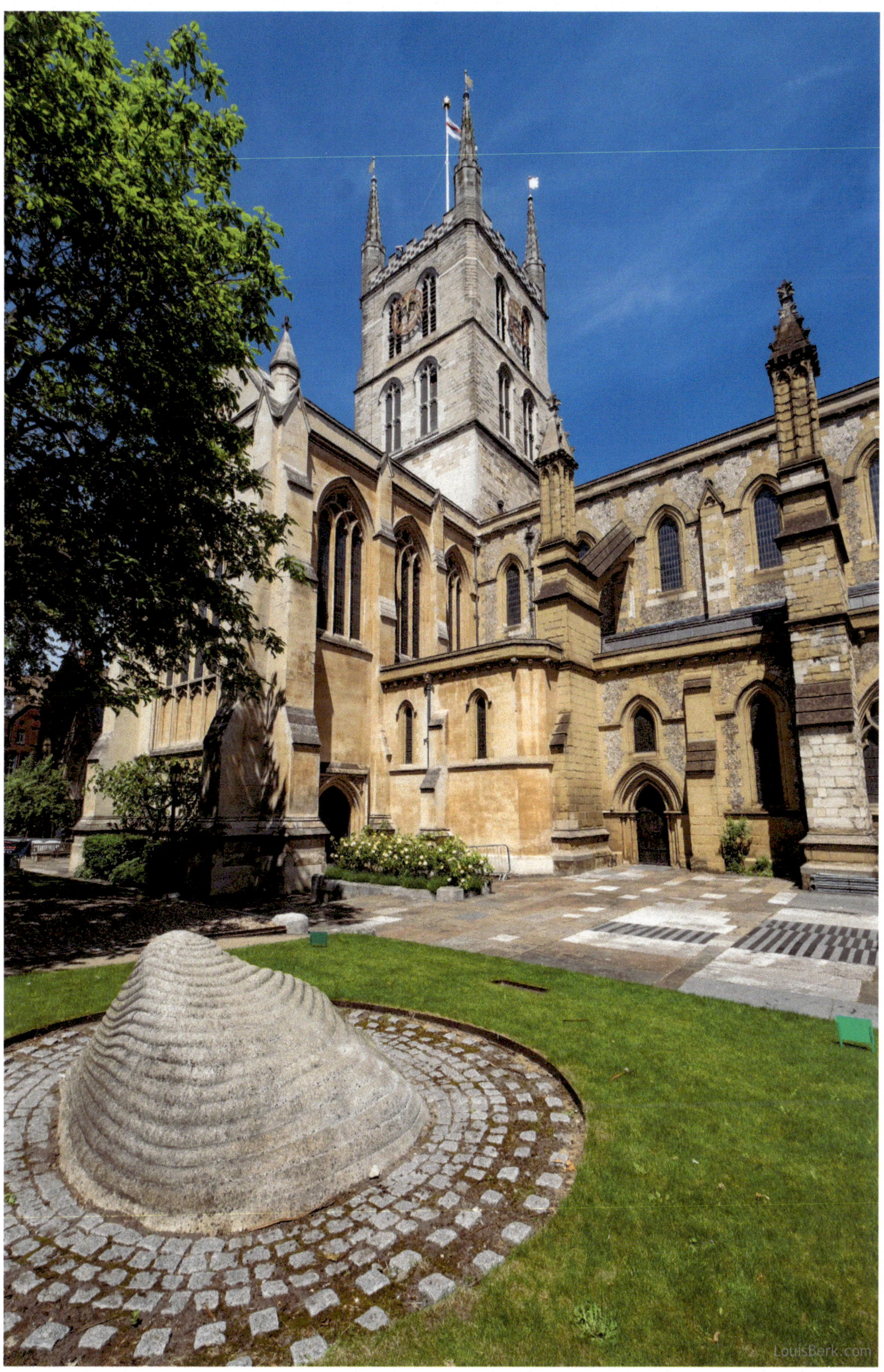

38. Borough Market

Visiting bustling Borough Market it is almost impossible that as recently as the late 1990s there was barely a public market here at all. It was the 1998 Food Lovers Fair with just fifty stalls that ushered in the revitalisation of empty buildings, previously a wholesale food market that relocated to Leyton in 1991 together with Spitalfields Market. Visitors were few but through word of mouth more produce and more gourmands arrived. By 1999 there were public food fairs once a quarter and then once a month, with the market eventually opening each week. Nowadays it is open daily with stalls selling fresh fish, meat, artisan baked goods, drinks, dairy produce and an array of condiments and sauces alongside cafés and independent outlets. The market is a series of three specialist areas: the Green Market for small traders, the Three Crown Market for larger food merchants and Borough Market Kitchen for hot street food. All are situated beneath railway lines and connected by passageways producing an intoxicating mix of sound, sights and, above all, taste.

A twenty-year master plan from 1995 included a double-height glass atrium fronting Borough High Street and the Floral Hall from Covent Garden. Built in 1860 as a flower market alongside the Royal Opera House, during the 1998 Opera House redevelopment one half of the Floral Hall was retained in situ with the other half offered to Borough Market for the notional price of £1. A new viaduct also pushed through the market in advance of London Bridge station's renovation (see Entry 42).

The mix of twenty-first-century delicacies, local workers, City financiers and tourists belies the market's long history. By the thirteenth century two markets were operating, one in the grounds of St Thomas's Hospital (see Entry 8) and the other along the approach to London Bridge. Later controlled by the City, local residents petitioned for their own market charter. The arrival of the South Eastern Railway in 1862 brought noise, dirt and a web of railway tracks but the market continued to expand. In the 1930s a set of art deco offices was erected, many of which survive. By 1933 the market was mostly wholesale servicing over eighty different companies but during the 1970s with the opening of New Covent Garden Market in Nine Elms and the rise of supermarkets, business slumped and relocation made economic sense but increased interest in food during the 1990s set the scene for Borough Market's renaissance.

Address: No. 8 Southwark Street, SE1 1TL
Built: 1851 – H. Rose; Refurbishment 1995/2015 – Greig and Stephenson Architects
Listed Status: Grade II (Floral Hall Portico)
Public Access: Yes
Tube/Rail: London Bridge
Website: boroughmarket.org.uk

Opposite: Floral Hall, Borough Market.

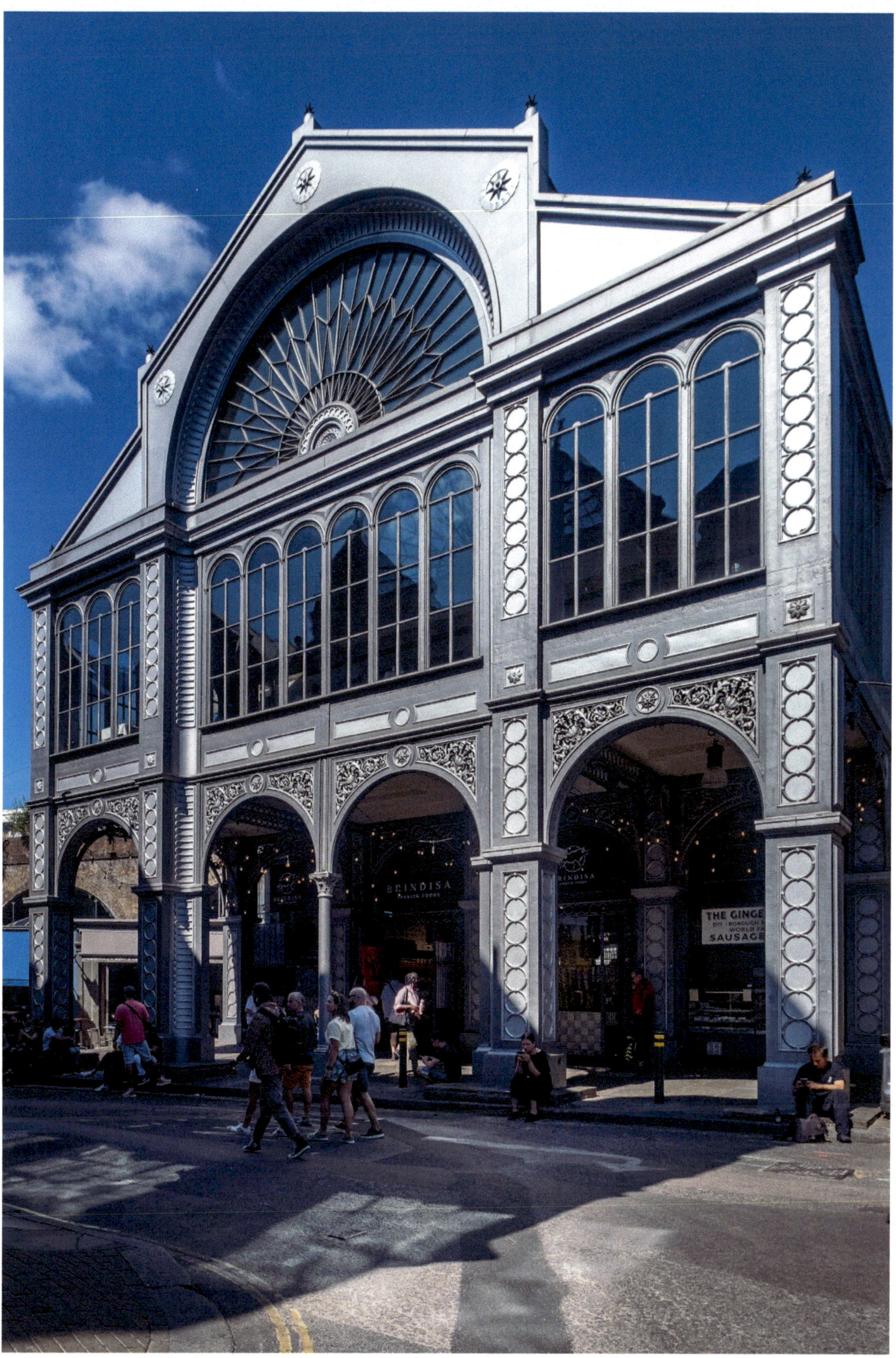

39. Glaziers' Hall

Of the 110 City of London livery companies, only the Worshipful Company of Glaziers and Painters of Glass has its hall south of the river, as it is alongside London Bridge, which is administered by the City. The Glaziers were first recorded in 1328, gaining their charter in 1637. Glass was made by fusing sand and limestone with wood ash but as wood became valuable for building ships, it was forbidden for glassmaking and coal ash was substituted. Ease of transporting coal on the River Thames allowed glass making to thrive and soon Southwark and Bankside were London's centre for producing bottles, drinking vessels and window panes, the latter though only for the wealthy.

The hall dates from 1808 but was substantially rebuilt as Hibernia Wharf following a warehouse fire in 1851. Designed by William Cubitt, who also built Hay's Wharf (see Entry 45), two floors of offices were incorporated with access from London Bridge, known today as Hibernia Chambers. In 1866 they were used by a specialised dairy company accessed directly from Montagu Close and stored perishable goods such as cheese and butter. Hibernia, a Latin name for Ireland, referenced the source of the produce. In the early 1900s cold storage facilities were added.

When the docks closed in 1970 the Co-Operative Society funded the redevelopment and the Glaziers relocated here having had no permanent home since the Great Fire of 1666. Paying a peppercorn rent of a shard of glass, the refurbished hall opened in 1978. Renovation in 2017 restored original Yorkshire stone flooring and stained glass windows, revealed brickwork in the entrance and reception areas and incorporated a wine cellar into one of the adjoining London Bridge arches.

The Worshipful Companies of Scientific Instrument Makers and of Launderers, two livery companies without permanent premises, also use the hall. Access back to London Bridge is via a stone staircase erroneously known as Nancy's Steps, with a plaque linking the neighbourhood to the murder of Nancy by Bill Sykes in Charles Dickens's *Oliver Twist*. At the base of the staircase is a Jubilee Walkway roundel (see Did You Know Box below).

Address: No. 9 Montague Close, SE1 9DD
Built: 1808 – William Cubitt
Listed Status: Grade II
Public Access: By arrangement
Tube/Rail: London Bridge
Website: glaziershall.co.uk

The Queen's Jubilee Walkways

In celebration of the Queen's Silver Jubilee in 1977 a 5-mile route was devised through central London from Leicester Square to Tower Hill linking historic sites on both sides of the river. In addition, some of the riverfront was granted public access for the first time. Engraved pavement roundels decorated with a crown and inscribed with Jubilee Walkway marked the route. In 2012, the Diamond Jubilee year, the walkway was extended to cover 60 kilometres, one for every year of the reign. It extended westwards towards Little Venice and eastwards to Stratford, site of the London 2012 Olympic Games, another iconic event of the same year. Named the Jubilee Greenway, its pavement roundels incorporate a crown, a laurel wreath and two diamonds. Several points along the routes have both plaques.

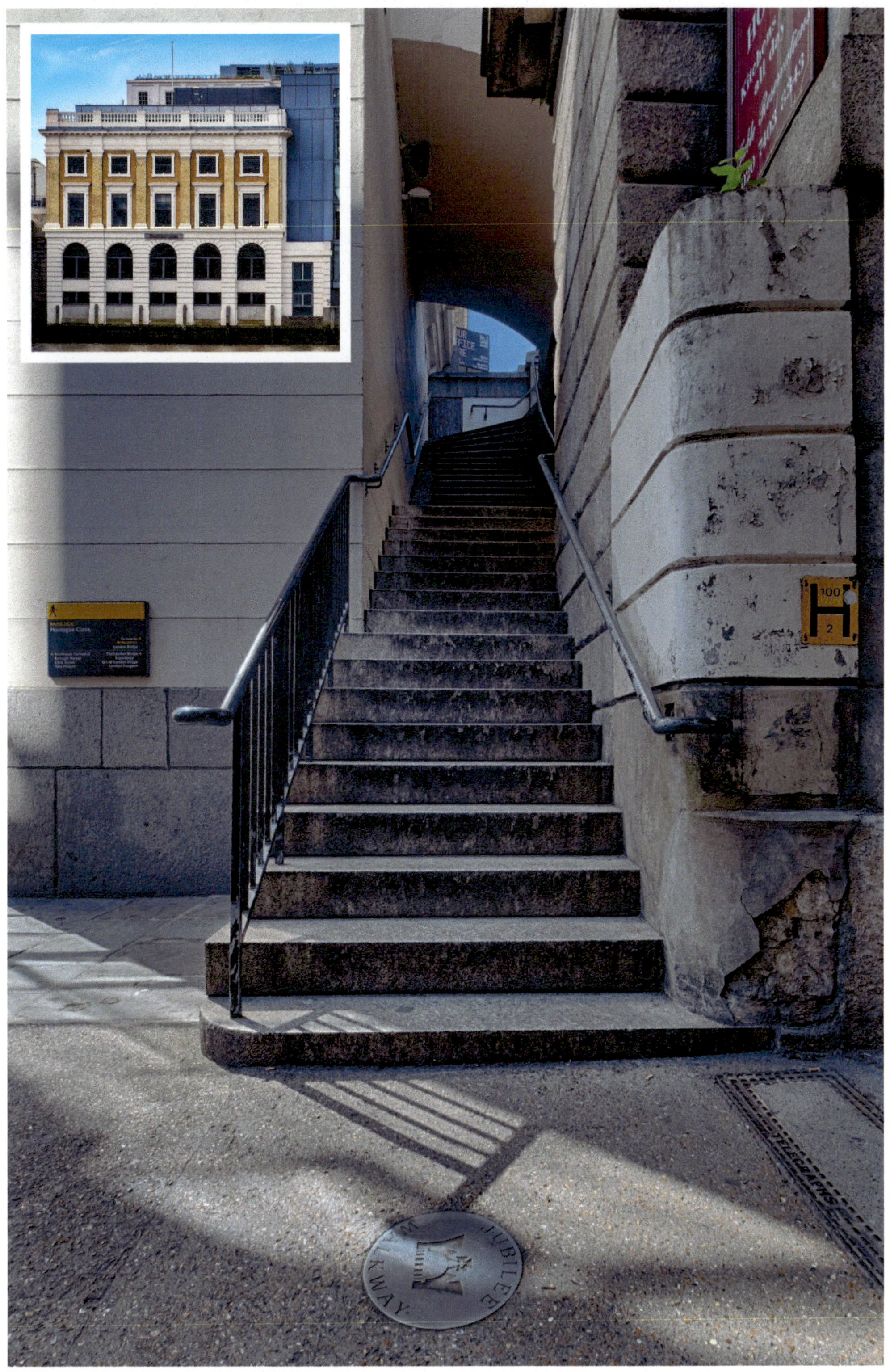

Nancy's Steps lead up to London Bridge. *Insert*: Glaziers' Hall.

40. No. 1 London Bridge

Resembling a giant cube with one side cut away, No. 1 London Bridge, the gateway to London Bridge City, is a postmodern building designed by John Bennington and completed in 1986. It sits on the site of Fennings Wharf, which had been rebuilt in 1836 following a fire and used to store wines and spirits and provide cold storage facilities. Later operated by Hay's Wharf Company, which owned much of the riverside between Tower and London Bridges, it closed in 1969, becoming the first part of a major redevelopment providing an impressive vista when looking across from the north bank.

The cube is thirteen storeys tall and linked to an adjoining ten-storey block by a five-storey building. High-level windows are angled to provide views westwards. Public walkways join the Thames Path (known here as Queen's Walk), Hay's Galleria (see Entry 45) and Tooley Street, integrating the building with the local streetscape. The building looks shiny

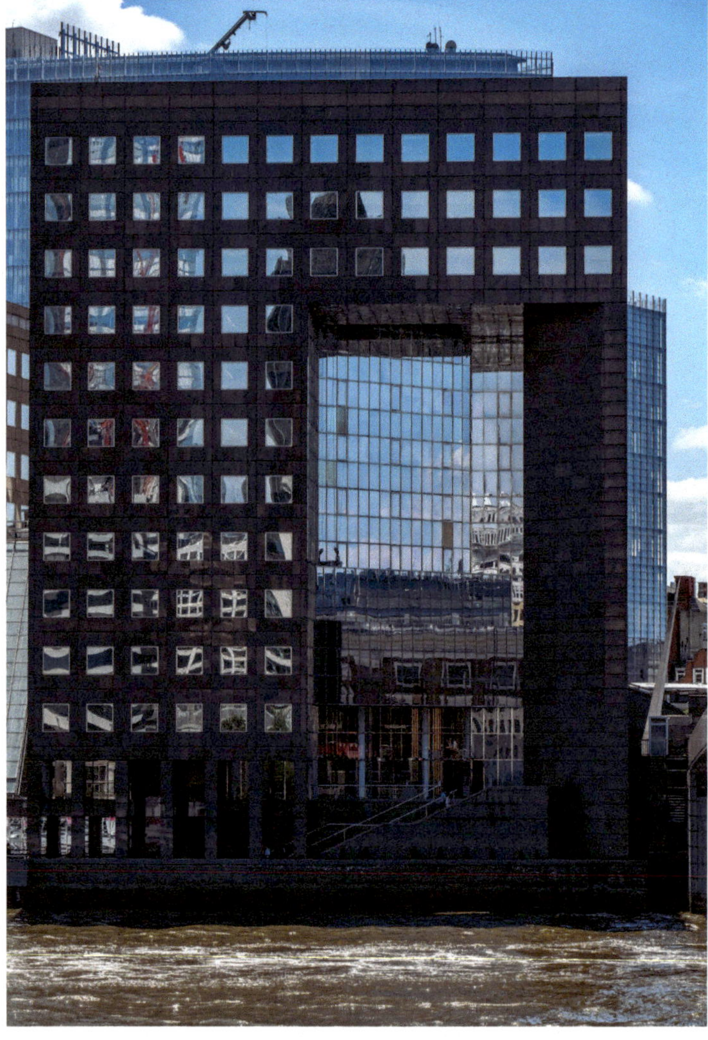

No. 1 London Bridge.

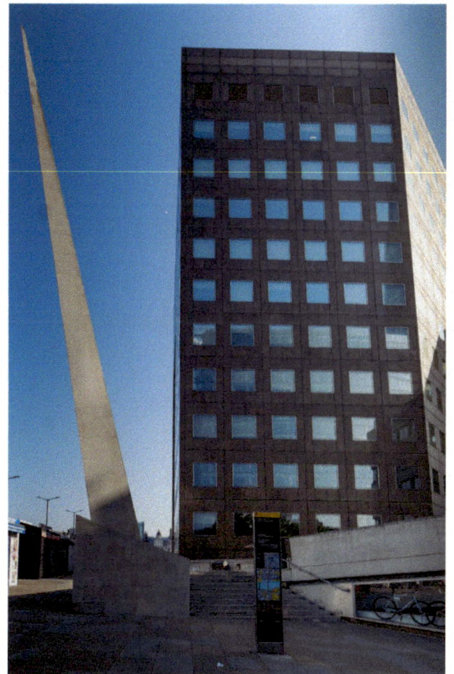

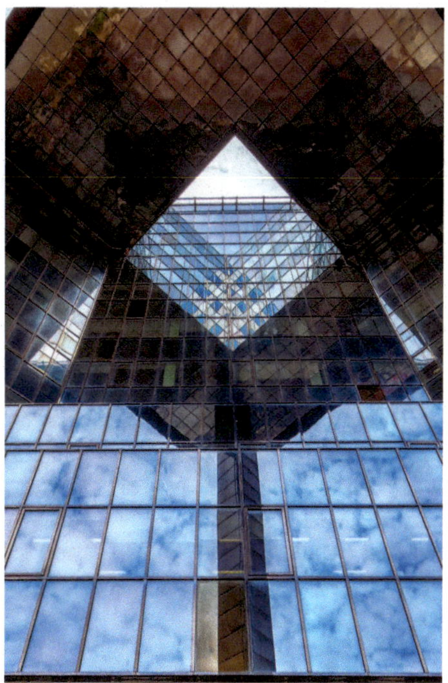

Above left: Southwark Spike.

Above right: Mirrored windows.

Right: City of London dragon.

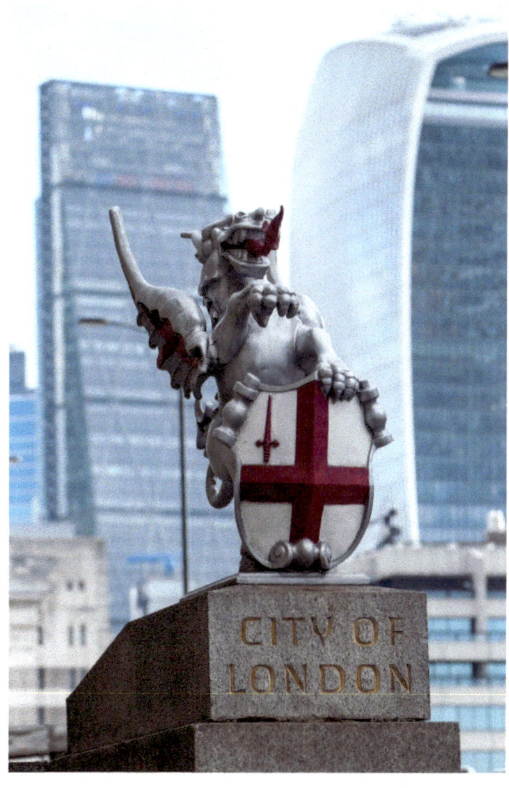

and bright due to the polished pink granite cladding and sleek stainless steel-clad window frames and columns.

The second stage of London Bridge City, with lead architects Michael Twigg, Brown & Partners, included the Cottons Centre, two nine-storey office blocks linked by a glass atrium built on the site of Cottons Wharf. The site, completed in 1988, includes large swathes of green glazing.

At the corner of Cottons Lane and Tooley Street is a memorial to James Braidwood, Superintendent of the London Fire Engine Establishment who died near this spot during the Great Fire of 1861. It features imagery of the fire with a fireman's axe and hose. A street named in his honour is towards the eastern end of Tooley Street.

Address: No. 1 London Bridge, SE1 9BA
Built: 1985/88 – John Bennington; Michael Twigg, Brown & Partners,
Public Access: No
Tube/Rail: London Bridge

City of London Dragon

Silver and red dragons form part of the City of London coat of arms but also mark various City boundaries. Following the 1963 demolition of the Coal Exchange, two cast-iron dragons were saved and relocated on the Embankment boundary of the Cities of London and Westminster. Half-size replicas were subsequently erected as boundary markers elsewhere in the City. They can be found in pairs at High Holborn and the south side of London Bridge and singly at Aldgate, Barbican, Blackfriars Bridge, Farringdon Street, Moorgate, Norton Folgate and Tower Hill.

Southwark Spike

This 16-metre tapered spear of Portland stone points southwards at an angle of 19.5 degrees marking the medieval gateway to Southwark. Commissioned by the LB Southwark and designed by architect Eric Parry, it is constructed from twenty-five separate blocks of stone. Resembling a compass point, it could also represent spikes used for displaying the heads of executed felons on the second London Bridge until King Charles II abolished the practice in 1660.

41. Old Operating Theatre Museum

A narrow wooden spiral staircase leads to the Old Operating Theatre Museum & Herb Garret, originally part of St Thomas's, one of London's oldest hospitals (see Entry 8). The hospital moved to Lambeth in 1862, making way for the South Eastern Railway (SER) extension from London Bridge to Charing Cross and the attic with its operating theatre was closed up and forgotten for nearly 100 years before being discovered in 1956, opening as a museum in 1962.

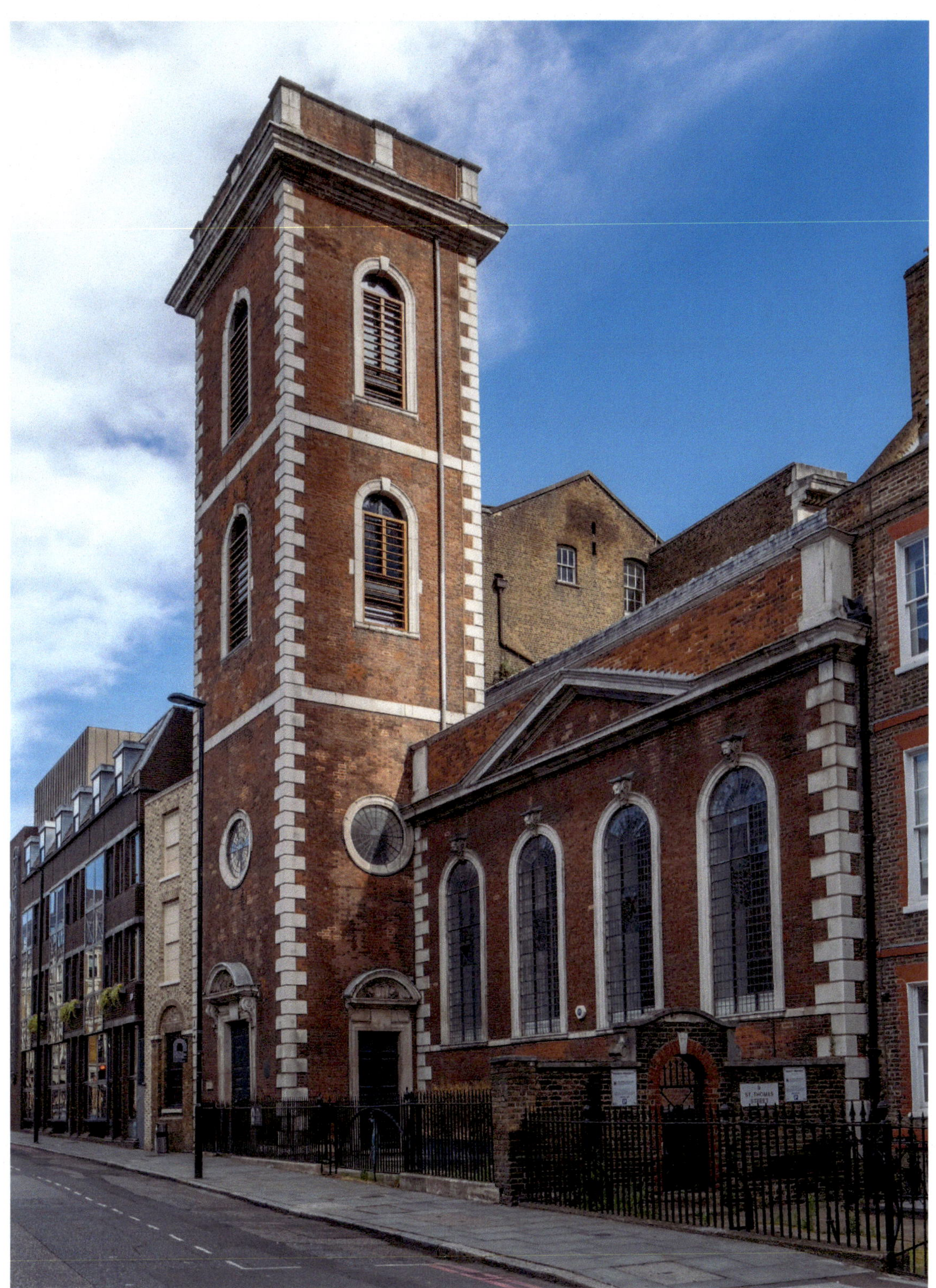

Old Operating Theatre Museum.

Founded in 1106 as part of the Augustinian Priory of St Mary Overie, now the site of Southwark Cathedral (see Entry 37), the hospital was later named in honour of Thomas Becket. By 1702 and further expansion the hospital included a new church dedicated to St Thomas the Apostle, all that survives of the original hospital. A women's operating theatre was incorporated into its attic in 1822. Florence Nightingale established her School of Nursing at St Thomas's, opening in 1860 with fifteen students.

Following relocation to Lambeth, most of the hospital was demolished, leaving only a block on Borough High Street now comprising St. Thomas's Church, which closed in 1898, and a post office.

When the entrance was discovered in 1956 it led to a dark, dusty, empty space with slates covering the skylight. Original fixtures remained indicating the theatre outline and, using a detailed SER inventory, a painstaking reconstruction commenced. Replica doors and a new skylight were installed, the original light yellow ochre colour scheme reinstated, and University College Hospital donated an early nineteenth-century operating table. Five semicircular stands rise steeply as this was, in effect, a real theatre and the show was an ordeal for both the medical students and the patient. With no anaesthetics until 1841 or antiseptics until the 1860s, pain was endured through drinking alcohol and biting into a piece of leather while held down by theatre assistants. The attic location prevented screams reaching patients awaiting surgery.

Between 1702 and 1822, hospital apothecaries stored and dried herbs in St Thomas's Church attic where today displays of medical instruments, early pill-making equipment and historical images of the hospital and the use of antiseptics and anaesthetics form an introduction to the operating theatre next door where an imaginative events programme covers all aspects of the theatre and medical developments in surgery, anaesthetics and hygiene.

Address: No. 9A St Thomas Street, SE1 9RY
Built: 1702
Listed Status: Grade II*
Public Access: Yes; entrance fee. Note: the staircase has fifty-two steps
Tube/Rail: London Bridge
Website: oldoperatingtheatre.com

42. London Bridge Station Viaduct

The arrival of the London & Greenwich Railway in 1836 followed by the London & Croydon Railway in 1839 transformed Tooley Street from a warehouse lined thoroughfare to one dominated by the railway viaduct, over 850 brick arches, linking London Bridge to Greenwich stations.

Following the 1960s docks closure the riverside developed into a linear commercial and residential neighbourhood (see Entries 40, 44, 45, 47, 48 and 49). The roadside has only recently been transformed with the 2013/18 redevelopment of London Bridge station. Until then the Tooley Street arches were grimy and dismal, albeit perfect for such attractions as the London Dungeons (now relocated) and the Britain at War Experience (now closed). The changes providing enhanced public access to the station were so dramatic that it was

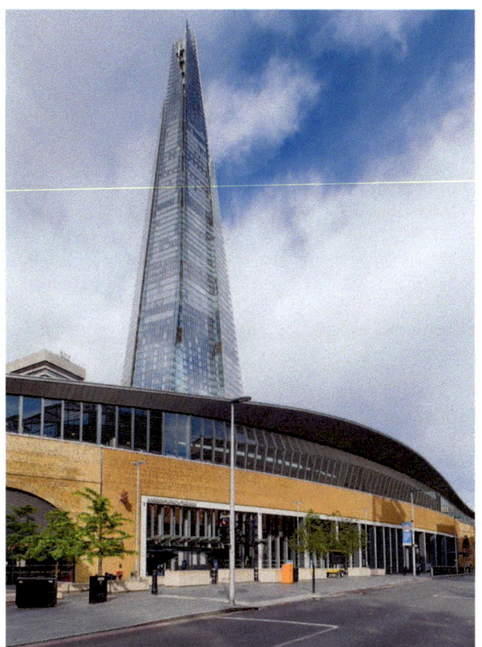

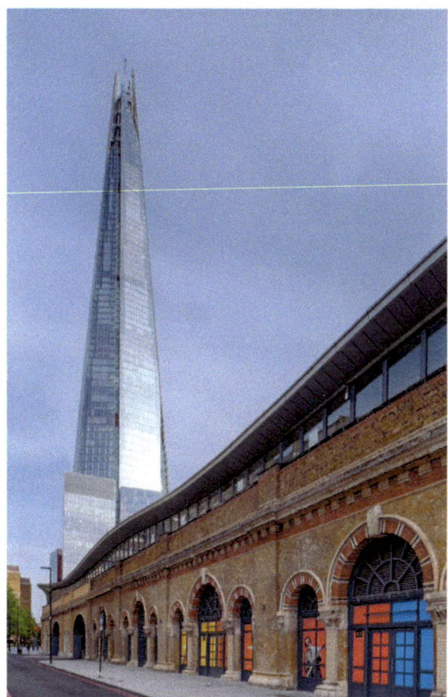

Above left and above right:
London Bridge station
redevelopment above the
Victorian railway viaduct.

Right: Decorative umbrellas,
Stainer Street.

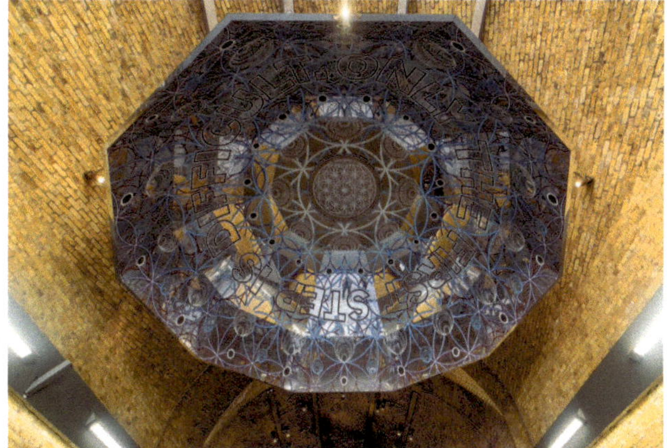

immediately difficult to remember how it used to look. Stainer Street, previously a dingy traffic thoroughfare, reopened in 2018 as a public walkway into the station.

The station redevelopment has a real 'wow' factor with extensive glazing to both sides, making a once dark and gloomy interior light and bright. Facilities including shops, ticket offices, barriers and seating are in close proximity and paired escalators lead to the platforms above with timber-clad ceilings below softening the aesthetics and sound. A display of archaeological discoveries made during excavations between 2012 and 2017 provide an insight into pre-railway Tooley Street, with items including twelfth-century floor tiles, chamber pots and toothbrushes. Another passageway leads to a row of renovated arches with retail outlets sympathetically inserted along both sides and the St Thomas Street side leads to The Shard (see Entry 43).

On Joiner Street an information plaque with the South East Railway insignia describes the 1839 viaduct, with the girder bridge above dating from 1849.

Address: Station Approach Road, SE1 9SP
Built: 1830s, extended late 1800s; Refurbishment 2013/18 – Grimshaw and Partners
Listed Status: Grade II (Platforms 9 to 16, Joiner Street Bridge)
Public Access: Yes
Tube/Rail: London Bridge
Website: networkrail.co.uk

43. The Shard

From almost any central London viewpoint, one building stands out more than any other, the tall slender tapering spire known as The Shard.

Built alongside London Bridge station (see Entry 42) and originally named London Bridge Tower, the nickname comes from the predominate building material and its shape resembling a shard of glass. Opened in 2012, it was built on the site of Southwark Towers, an outdated 1975 office block demolished in 2008 having been the headquarters of accountancy firm PricewaterhouseCoopers (PwC). Regeneration plans for the neighbourhood were already well underway but The Shard has since become the symbol for this previously unloved area.

Designed by Italian architect Renzo Piano in association with property developer Irvine Sellar, The Shard is 310 metres high. Once the tallest building in Europe, it is now the seventh but remains the tallest in the UK. Opened to the public in February 2013, visitors were immediately attracted to the viewing areas between floors 68 and 72 where views on a clear day reach over 64 kilometres.

Irvine Sellar envisaged the notion of a vertical town providing residential, commercial and hospitality facilities. The Shard fulfilled his brief with, from the ground up, twenty floors of office space, restaurants on floors 31 to 33, the luxury Shangri La Hotel occupying the 34th to 52nd floors, and thirteen floors of apartments above. A fifteen-level spire rising from the 72nd floor provided that extra bit of height required for the record books but its deliberately jagged edge is often mistaken for the structure being unfinished.

It is extremely environmentally friendly with 95 per cent of building materials recycled and the exterior incorporating 11,000 panes of reflective glass shimmers variously depending on the season and time of day. Shard Plaza at ground level offers a public seating area, integrating the structure into St Thomas Street, and a second floor retail area leads directly to London Bridge station. For many, The Shard looming over neighbouring social housing estates confirms the gulf between different communities, but for others it is a helpful visual clue to south London's location.

Address: No. 32 London Bridge Street, SE1 9SG
Built: 2009/13 – Renzo Piano
Public Access: Yes; entrance fee
Tube/Rail: London Bridge
Website: the-shard.com

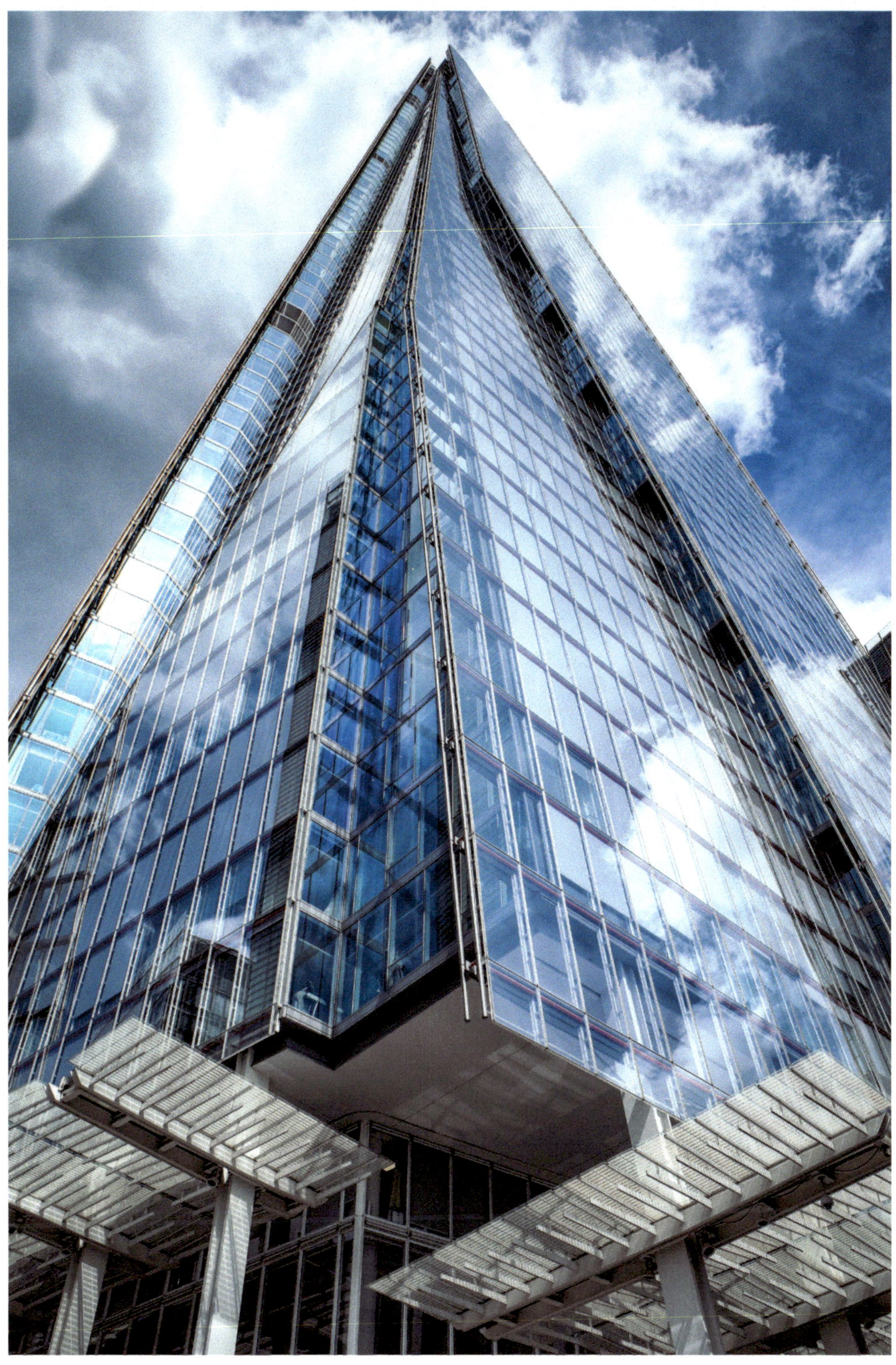

View of The Shard from its base.

44. St Olaf House and London Bridge Hospital

The art deco gem of St Olaf House, nestling between 1980s redevelopments, currently houses the administration centre and consulting rooms for London Bridge Hospital. Designed by Henry Stuart Goodhart-Rendel, a soldier, composer, pianist, author and architect, St Olaf House was built between 1929 and 1931 as the Hay's Wharf Company headquarters. A black and gold mosaic of St Olaf commemorates the Church of St Olave Bermondsey, previously on this site and one of four churches in Bermondsey and the City of London, named in honour of King (later Saint) Olaf, who assisted with the pulling down of London Bridge in 1014, defending London against the invading Danes.

Built of Portland stone around a steel frame, the T shape of the building is not immediately evident but the stalk of the T leads to the riverfront with the crosspiece on

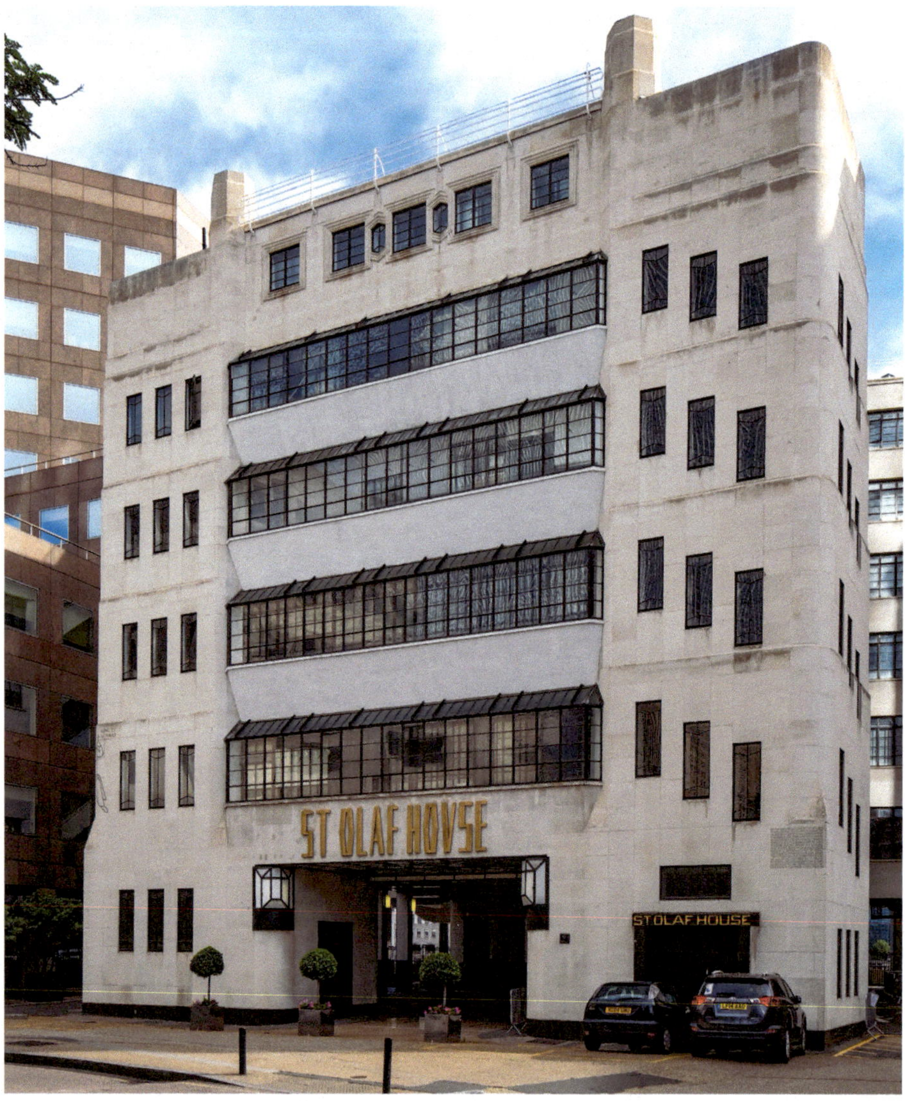

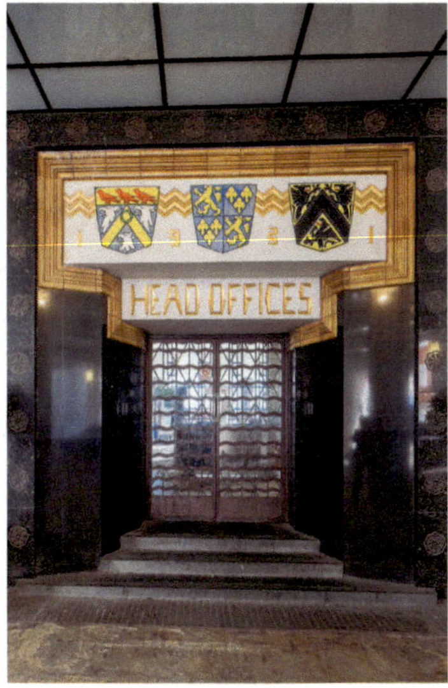
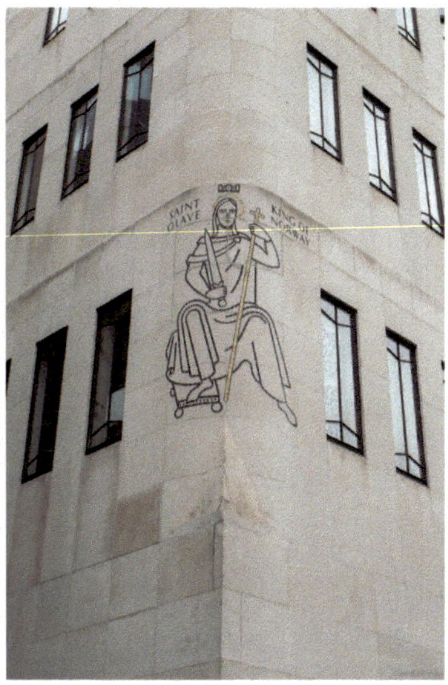

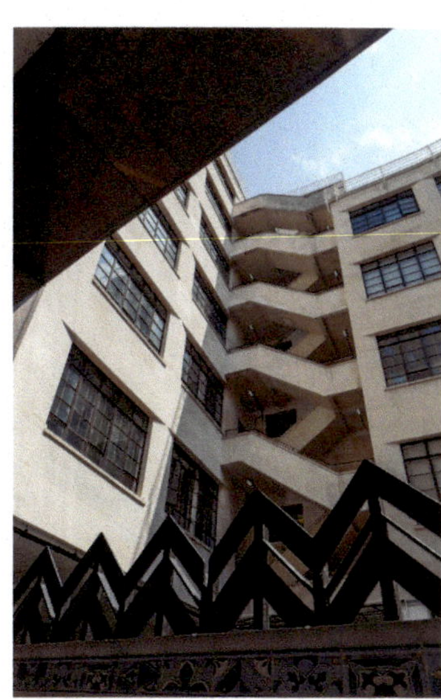

Opposite and above: St Olaf House.

Tooley Street. Decoration includes slim lettering, different-shaped windows and bronze light fittings. The building stands on 'legs' facilitating riverside access.

The decorative riverfront fascia is a reminder of when warehouses, wharves and offices linked to the docks were mainly visible from the River Thames. The golden and terracotta relief, Capital, Labour and Commerce, was fashioned by Frank Dobson (see Entry 16). Hay's Wharf in gilt lettering at roof level advertised the company to the Pool of London, the docks between London and Tower Bridges nicknamed London's Larder due to the amount of breakfast produce – bacon, cheese and butter – being handled. Bands of black granite mark the position of the original boardroom and directors' common room.

Following the closure of the docks, the building underwent extensive restoration between 1982 and 1983 for occupation by actuarial firm Bacon & Woodrow, which relocated to More London (see Entry 47) in 2006. London Bridge Hospital, a private medical care company established next door in 1986, then extended into St Olaf House.

London Bridge Hospital opened in the converted 1860s Chamberlain Wharf, which had primarily handled potatoes. It was repurposed in 1985 by Llewellyn-Davies Weeks incorporating a glass barrelled atrium. Walkways link to Denmark and Emblem Houses, both dockland storage facilities converted into hospital departments. Exterior detailing of anchors, fish and tridents on Denmark House reminds visitors of the building's previous activity. No. 33 Tooley Street, once shipping offices, completes the extensive hospital complex.

Address: No. 27 Tooley Street, SE1 2PR
Built: 1928/32 – H. S. Goodhart-Rendel
Listed Status: Grade II*
Public Access: No
Tube/Rail: London Bridge
Website: hcahealthcare.co.uk/facilities/london-bridge-hospital

45. Hay's Galleria

On the site of Hay's Dock, the Galleria is a series of office blocks where Tea Auction, Counting and Shackleton Houses evoke trading and exploration history. Access via Tooley Street or the riverside leads visitors to the Galleria, once a seventeenth-century dock named after Alexander Hay, who acquired the Tooley Street Brewery in 1651 and after whom a pub has been named. The estate expanded to become a complex of six-storey warehouses and small inland dock designed and built in 1856 by Sir William Cubitt for the then owner, John Humphrey. They were swiftly rebuilt following the 1861 Tooley Street fire and the Hay's Wharf company lost 14 per cent of their capacity during the Blitz before again rebuilding. By the 1960s the estate owned 38 acres of wharves, cold storage facilities and warehouses. Its closure in 1970 with the demise of London's docks belies the fact that just two years earlier there were still over 5,000 employees at Hay's.

One of the first redeveloped dockland sites, it reopened in 1987 with the curved atrium covered by a glass roof designed by Michael Twigg, Brown and Partners. Post-war warehouses were replaced by Victorian-style buildings for residential accommodation and offices. The original dock was drained and repurposed as an underground car park.

The space is dominated by a vast 18-metre-long kinetic bronze sculpture, *The Navigators*, sitting in a pool of water. Designed by David Kemp, it resembles a giant ship but is actually humanoid with the face of a man and the body of a trading ship with oars that move when the sculpture is operated.

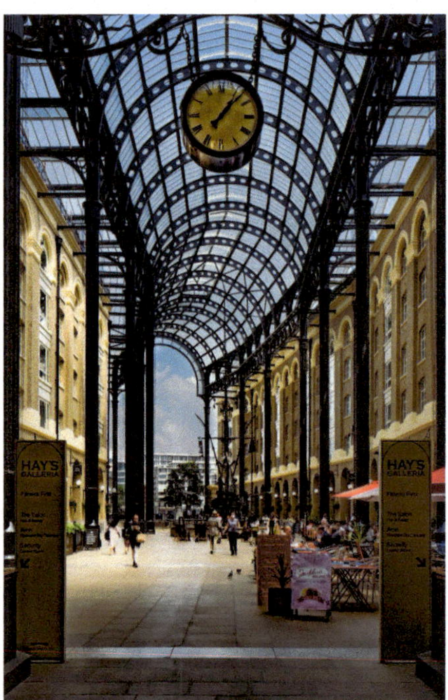

Atrium of Hay's Galleria.

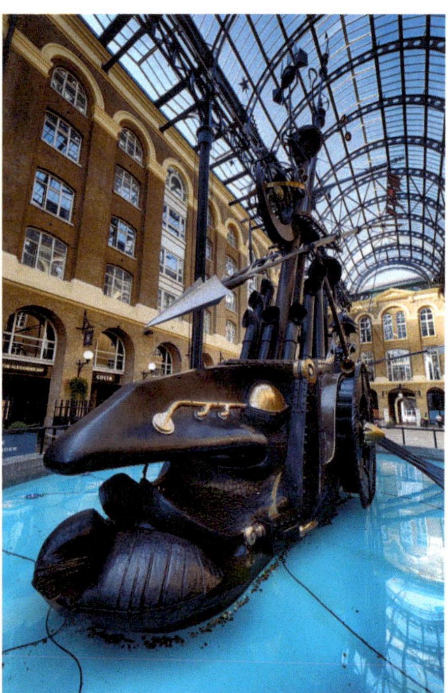

The Navigators by David Kemp.

A plaque on the corner of Tooley Street and Battle Bridge Lane commemorates the Great Fire of 1861, which blazed for two weeks due to the immense amount of inflammable goods stored. More lives were lost in this fire than the Great Fire of 1666, including that of James Braidwood, superintendent of the London Fire Engine Establishment. This fire led to the founding, in 1866, of what is now the London Fire Brigade (see Entry 4). A separate memorial to Braidwood is on the corner of Cottons Lane (see Entry 40).

Address: No. 1 Battle Bridge Lane, SE1 2HD
Built: 1861 – William Cubitt ; refurbishment twentieth century – Michael Twigg, Brown and Partners
Listed Status: Grade II
Public Access: Yes
Tube/Rail: London Bridge
Website: hays-galleria.com

46. HMS *Belfast*

Dominating the Thames approaching Tower Bridge is HMS *Belfast*, a twentieth-century warship which, since retirement from service in the 1960s, is permanently moored as part of the Imperial War Museum (IWM).

Built by Harland & Wolff in Belfast, hence the name, and launched in 1938, it was one of the last and, at 11,500 tons, one of the largest of the Royal Navy battle cruisers. She began Second World War service almost immediately, guarding Arctic convoys of supplies

HMS *Belfast* moored close to Tower Bridge.

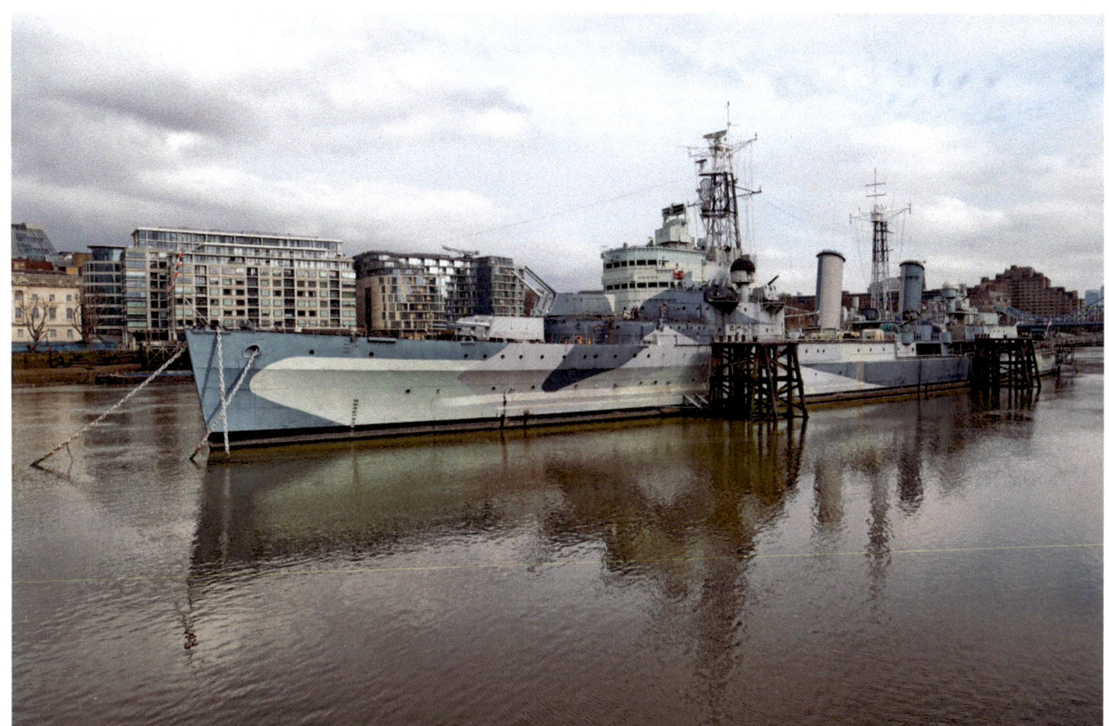

and capturing a German ship, the *Cap Norte*. Subsequent mine damage saw her out of action until 1942 before serving again at the North Cape in 1943 and Normandy in 1944. She is the only remaining British D-Day bombardment vessel. She later saw service during the 1950s Korean War and her current camouflage, pale and dark grey with pale blue wide stripes at random angles, dates from that time.

From 1966 the *Belfast* was used as an accommodation ship, and plans were made for its disposal. A group at the IWM established a charitable trust to preserve it and after an extensive and costly renovation it was opened to the public on 21 October (Trafalgar Day) 1971.

Flags flying from the taller of the two masts are International Maritime Signals indicating the pennant number (C35 for Cruiser 35) and call sign (GGCN). There are nine decks to explore via several narrow, steep ladders, bringing to life not only her military duties but also life on board for the 800 crew. Visitors can compare officers' bunks to sailors' hammocks and find the brass line on deck demarcating the officers-only section, a reminder of strict delineation of rank. The kitchen galley and hospital quarters are popular displays alongside the armoury room lined with 6-inch (wooden replica) shells ready to be raised to the gun turret.

Address: The Queen's Walk, SE1 2JH
Built: 1938
Public Access: Yes; entrance fee
Tube/Rail: London Bridge, Tower Hill
Website: iwm.org.uk/visits/hms-belfast

47. More London

More London, a new group of offices, housing, retail outlets and performance spaces, fills 13.5 acres between Hay's Galleria and City Hall (see Entries 45 and 48). Bordered by Tooley Street and Queen's Walk, it transformed what was, until recently, an area of Victorian houses and warehouses. The ambitious scheme by John Bennington with Michael Twigg, Brown and Partners (see Entries 36, 40 and 45) was originally called More London Bridge City but between 2000 and 2010, the shorter More London was adopted.

The accountancy firm PricewaterhouseCoopers (PwC), previously at the site of The Shard (see Entry 43), relocated to No. 7 More London, a dramatic ten-storey black glazed horseshoe-shaped office block designed by Foster + Partners. The open end faces the river. There is no obvious back and front, but a drop to seven storeys towards Tooley Street prevents the building overshadowing the streetscape. To many it resembles a helmet for a sci-fi movie character with its angled office wings resembling giant ears. Glazed bridges link the wings at various levels facilitating access for employees within the building.

Between No. 7 and the river are dancing fountains and The Scoop, a sunken stone open-air performance space with seating for over 800 people. Nearby, the Unicorn Theatre, a live entertainment venue, serves youth audiences. Founded in 1947 as the Caryl Jenner Mobile Theatre and renamed in 1962, the redevelopment provided an opportunity for a new purpose-built theatre, which opened in 2005. Also within the estate is Southwark Crown Court, formerly the site of Wilson's Wharf.

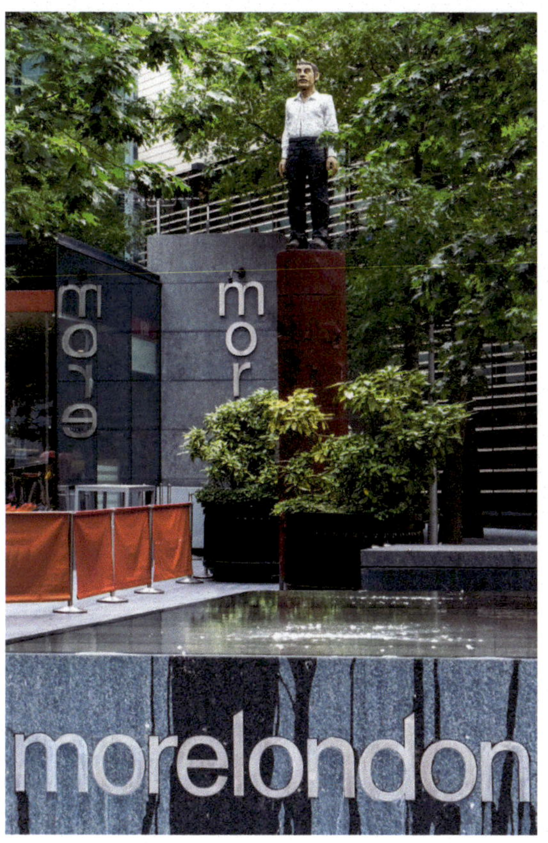

More London entrance, Tooley Street.

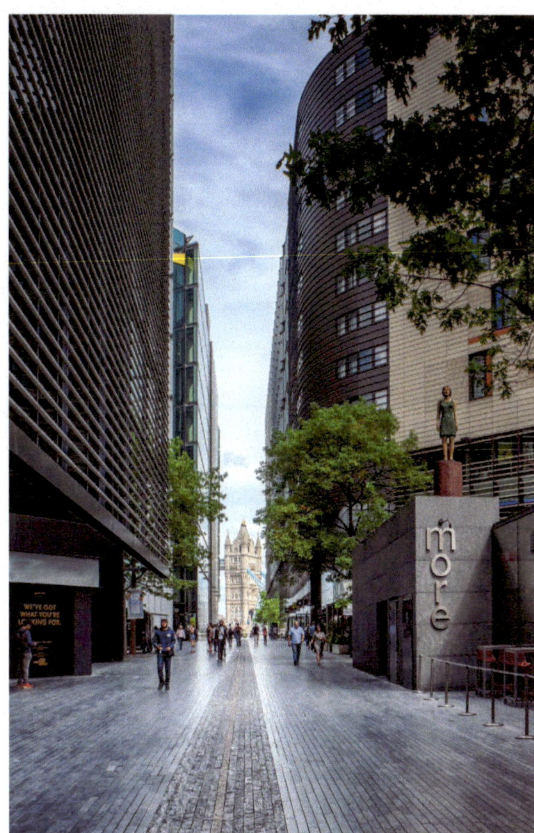

More London aligned with Tower Bridge.

At the western end a giant wooden sculpture of a man stands on a plinth. Designed by Stephan Balkenhol, he is one half of *Couple* with the female placed some distance away.

Between 2002 and 2018, a 600-metre narrow waterway named The Rill trickled between limestone paving stones but was filled in, renamed The Merchant Line and unveiled during the 2021 lockdown as a series of inlaid lettering along a metal line listing products and ports linked to the docks.

Address: Tooley Street, SE1 2RT
Built: Various
Public Access: External areas only
Tube/Rail: London Bridge, Tower Hill
Website: londonbridgecity.co.uk

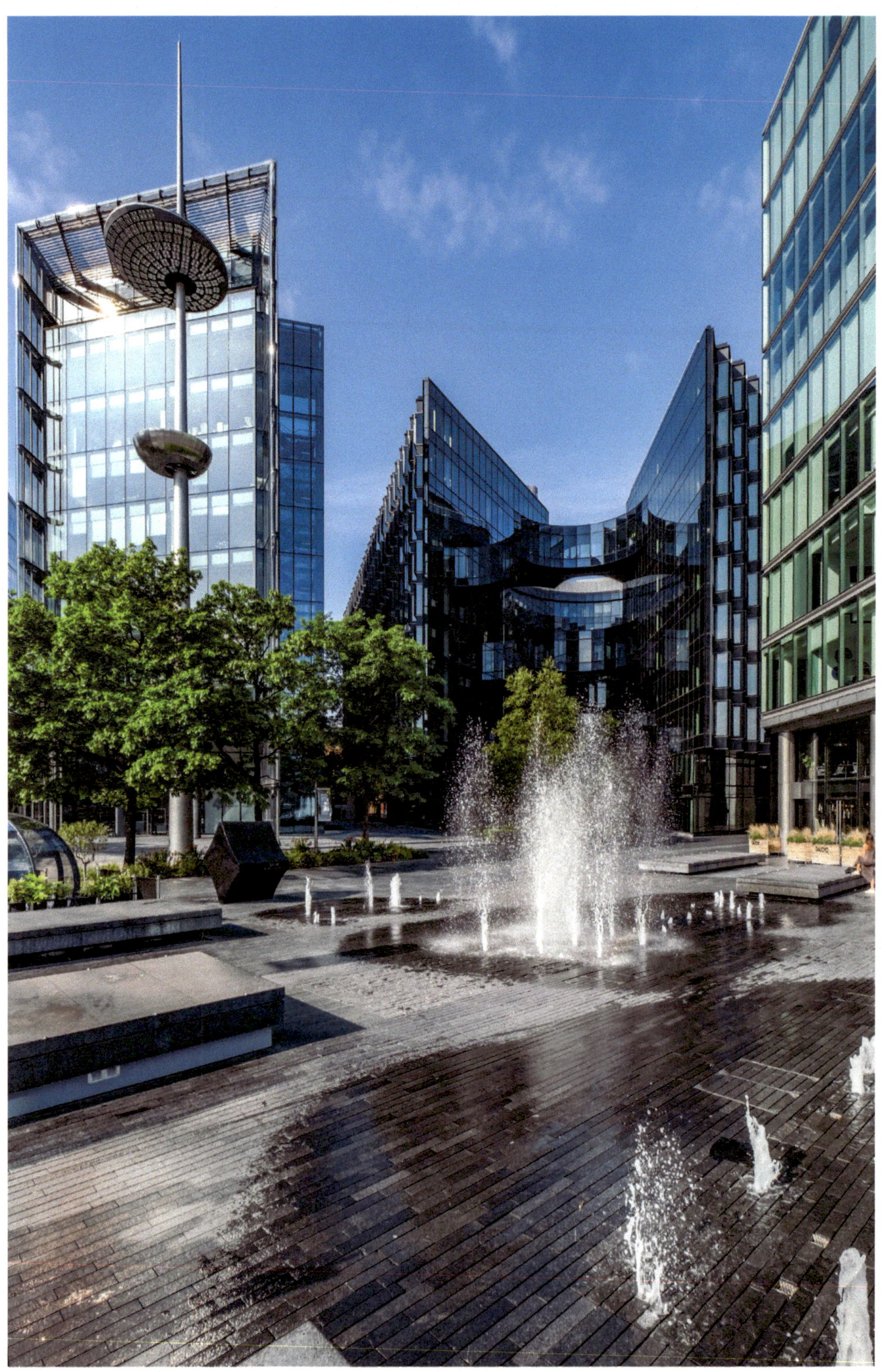

Water features and No. 7 More London.

48. City Hall

City Hall, built as the headquarters of the Greater London Authority (GLA), has been affectionately known as 'The Egg', 'The Pile of Plates' and 'The Headlamp'. Designed by Foster + Partners and completed in 2002, it occupies Potters Fields, a location of seventeenth-century London potteries. The area later became filled with wharves and warehouses and following the closure of the docks the site was included in plans for an ecological park. However, by the end of the twentieth century with plans for City Hall underway the area remained an open, rather desolate space.

The GLA, created in 2000, succeeded the Greater London Council (GLC), which managed London from County Hall (see Entry 10) from 1965 until its abolition in 1986. During the intervening years there was no overall governing body for London, home by 2000 to over 7 million residents. The GLA is a body of elected representatives headed by the Mayor of London. Ken Livingstone, once Leader of the GLC, was the first, elected in 2000, followed by Boris Johnson and Sadiq Khan.

The ten-storey building was considered unorthodox but the bulbous shape was heralded as energy efficient. There is no back, front or side elevation and the building was opened to the public with a spiral walkway linking the Council Chamber at the bottom to panoramic views from 'London's Living Room' at the top. En route visitors could see into the interior, including the Council Chamber, representing transparency of the organisation.

Its iconic shape and position has made it a film star, appearing in *Love Actually* and the twenty-fourth James Bond film *Spectre*.

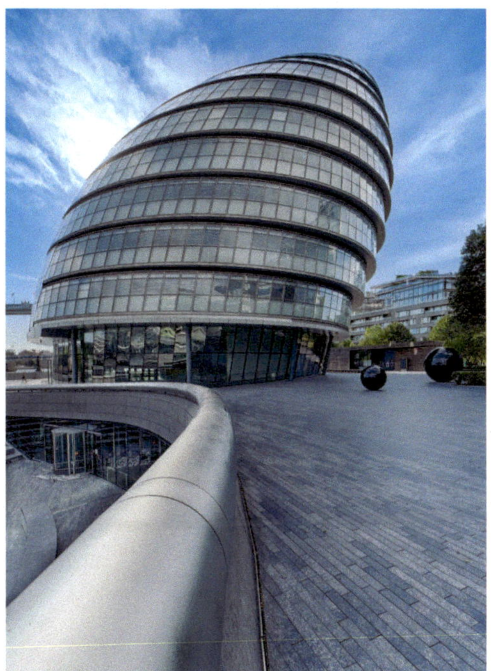

City Hall.

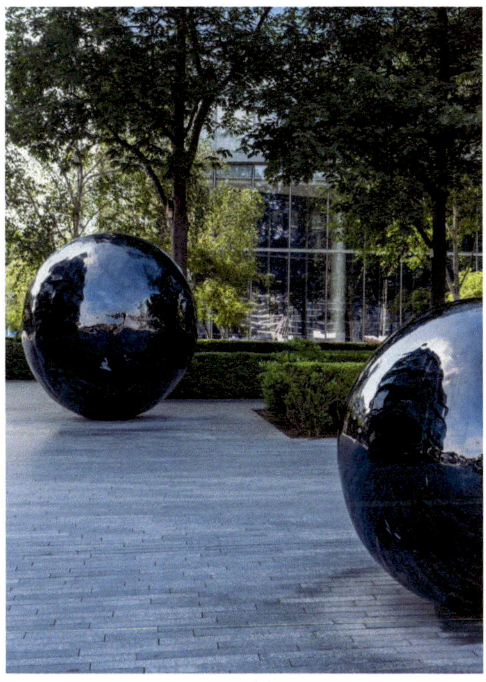

Reflecting sculptures.

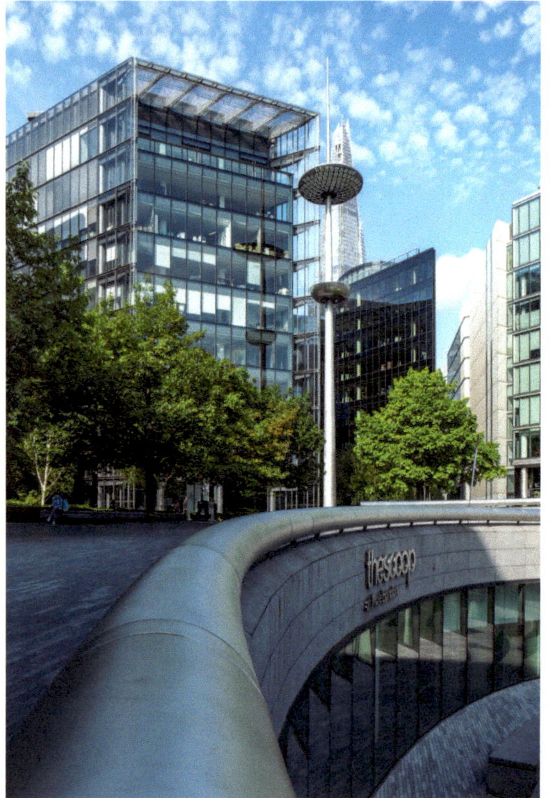

The Scoop.

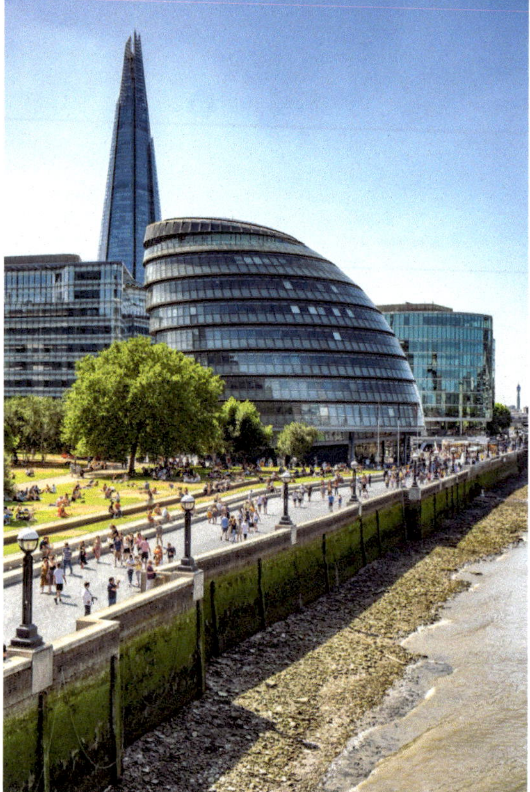

City Hall and More London from Tower Bridge.

In March 2022 the GLA moved to the repurposed Crystal site at Royal Victoria Docks. Leaving central London was controversial and at the time of writing, City Hall is empty, awaiting a new occupier and likely a new name too.

Address: No. 110 The Queen's Walk, SE1 2AA
Built: 1999/2002 – Foster + Partners
Tube/Rail: London Bridge, Tower Hill
Website: london.gov.uk

49. Bridge Theatre

Embedded in One Tower Bridge, a new residential block, large bright red letters proclaim Bridge Theatre, indicating clearly both location and purpose.

Opened in 2017 for the London Theatre Company, this award-winning performance space occupies the ground floor and basement and is the second largest theatre in the LB Southwark after the Globe (see Entry 30).

The wide glass frontage broken up by three bare concrete pillars leads to a light spacious foyer. Felt banners lining the ceiling facilitate excellent acoustics, creating a 'buzz' in the foyer but allowing for private conversation too. The density of the felting cleverly reduces sound as theatregoers approach the auditorium, ushering the 'expectant hush' of a theatre experience. Likewise, the foyer narrows towards the staircase acting as a gentle funnel to the interior. A dark timber staircase with wide shallow steps leading theatregoers to the stalls contrasts with the light oak handrail and different timbers used for the bar, flooring and shelving. Lighting is provided by 500 light fittings wrapped within a fine copper mesh emulating crumpled handkerchiefs.

Designed by Haworth Tompkins, specialists in theatre building and restoration projects, the performance space is large but flexible, making it suitable for all production types.

Leaving the building brings unparalleled views of the City, Tower of London and Tower Bridge (see Entry 50).

To the left and left again on exiting One Tower Bridge is a small public square with a statue of Sir Simon Milton looking towards City Hall (see Entry 48) where he worked as deputy Mayor of London between 2008 and 2011. He died at the age of forty-nine.

Address: No. 3 Potters Fields Park, SE1 2SG
Built: 2017 – Haworth Tompkins
Public Access: Yes
Tube/Rail: London Bridge, Tower Hill
Website: bridgetheatre.co.uk

Bridge Theatre at night. (© Mark Petersen)

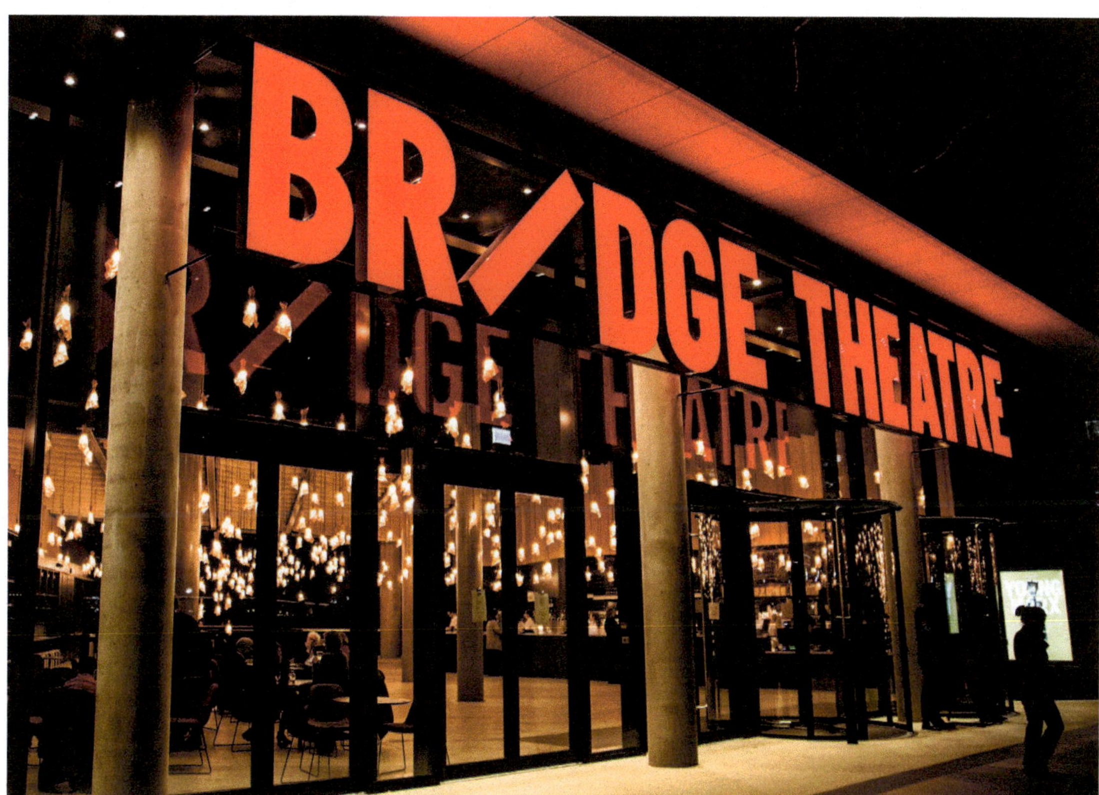

50. Tower Bridge

One of London's most iconic symbols, Tower Bridge is much younger than it looks. Opened in 1894, its Victorian Gothic style complemented the Tower of London, from which it takes its name. By the mid-nineteenth century traffic to and from the docks, wharves and warehouses in the Pool of London was increasing. At that time the most easterly bridge was London Bridge, with an underwater tunnel further east linking Wapping with Rotherhithe.

A design competition for the new bridge was won in 1884 by City of London architect Sir Horace Jones and engineer John Wolfe Barry. The steel framework is clad with Cornish granite and Portland stone. Originally painted a dull brown the bridge was redecorated in 1977 in red, white and blue for the Queen's Silver Jubilee. When a tall ship needs to enter the Pool of London the bridge, originally using hydraulic power, splits open, the bascules rising to angles of 83 degrees. Since 1976 electric- and oil-driven engines have been used. The bridge takes five minutes to rise and, on average, opens 850 times per year. In 1894 it opened over 6,000 times, indicating the change in river use. Bridge openings are arranged free of charge for any ship, provided twenty-four-hour notice is received with the Bridge Risings schedule publicly available. The two square towers, both 65 metres high, linked by high-level walkways, allowed pedestrians to continue crossing when the bridge below was raised. However, they soon became the haunts of footpads (thieves) and prostitutes and in

Tower Bridge is raised for a Thames sailing barge.

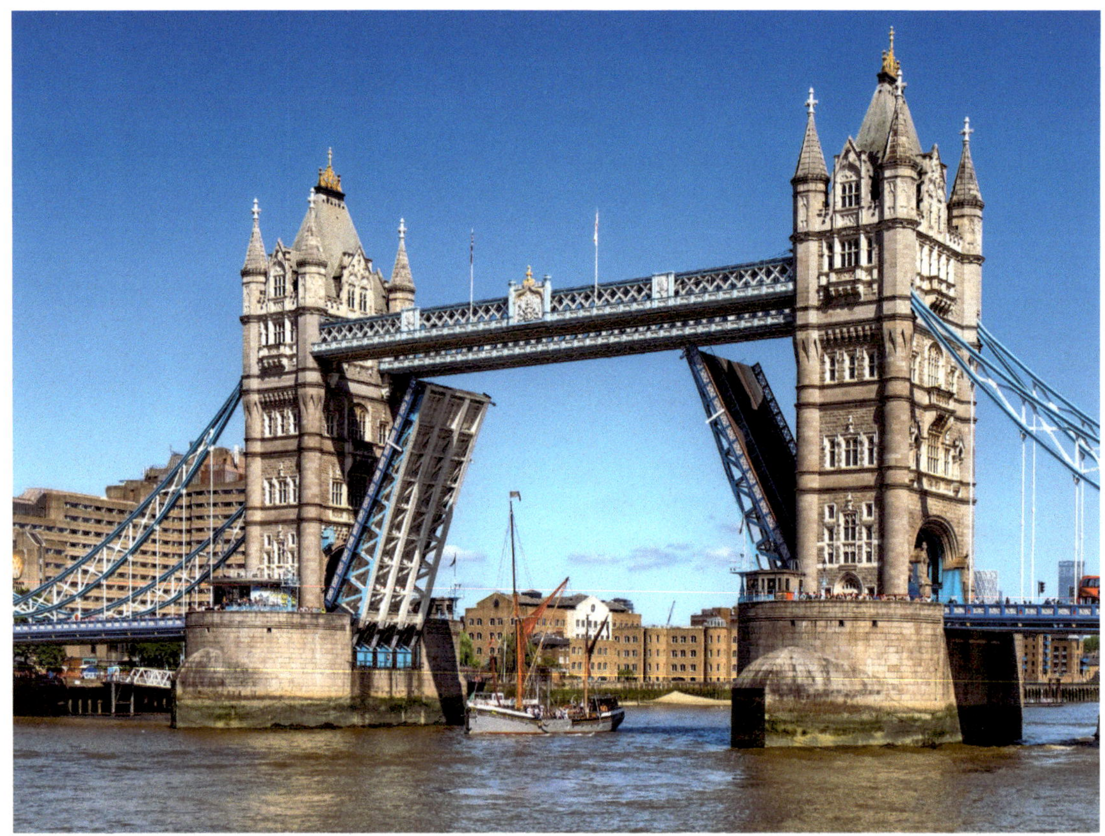

1910 were closed to the public. They reopened in 1982 as a visitor attraction together with the engine room on the south bank. In 2014 glass floors were installed in the walkways providing a bird's-eye view of the river, as well as magnificent vistas eastwards to Canary Wharf and westwards across to the City, the south bank and beyond.

Seen regularly in films to place the action firmly in London, the most famous image is likely that from 30 December 1952 when a bus leapt from one bascule to the other.

Address: Tower Bridge Road, SE1 2UP
Built: 1886/94 – John Wolfe Barry, Horace Jones
Listed Status: Grade I
Public Access: Yes; entrance fee for visitor attraction
Tube/Rail: London Bridge, Tower Hill
Website: towerbridge.org.uk

About the Authors and Acknowledgements

Louis Berk

Professional photographer and author Louis Berk (www.louisberk.com) has collaborated with Rachel on three books, *Whitechapel in 50 Buildings*, *Secret Whitechapel* and *Whitechapel Doors*. As a photographer he is the author of *East End Jewish* Cemeteries and *Primrose Hill: The London Stage*. Since 2019 he has been the project photographer for the lottery-funded Bevis Marks Synagogue Heritage Foundation. His work is often seen in print and online publications and when not looking after his five cats his passion is wildlife photography, especially London's urban foxes.

Rachel Kolsky

Engaging, knowledgeable and entertaining, Rachel is a popular London Blue Badge Tourist Guide (www.golondontours.com) whose walks and talks focus on the 'human stories behind the buildings'. She was a Trustee of The Phoenix, her local independent cinema, for over twenty years, has published several books including *Jewish London* and *Women's London* and has been a guest lecturer on cruises since 2009.

Acknowledgements

The authors would like to thank Amberley for commissioning this book and also acknowledge the following individuals for their assistance and use of images: Amir Paivar, Shell Centre; Mark Petersen for his Bridge Theatre photograph; Monica Walker, Old Operating Theatre Museum; and Rosalind Zeffertt for her invaluable advice.

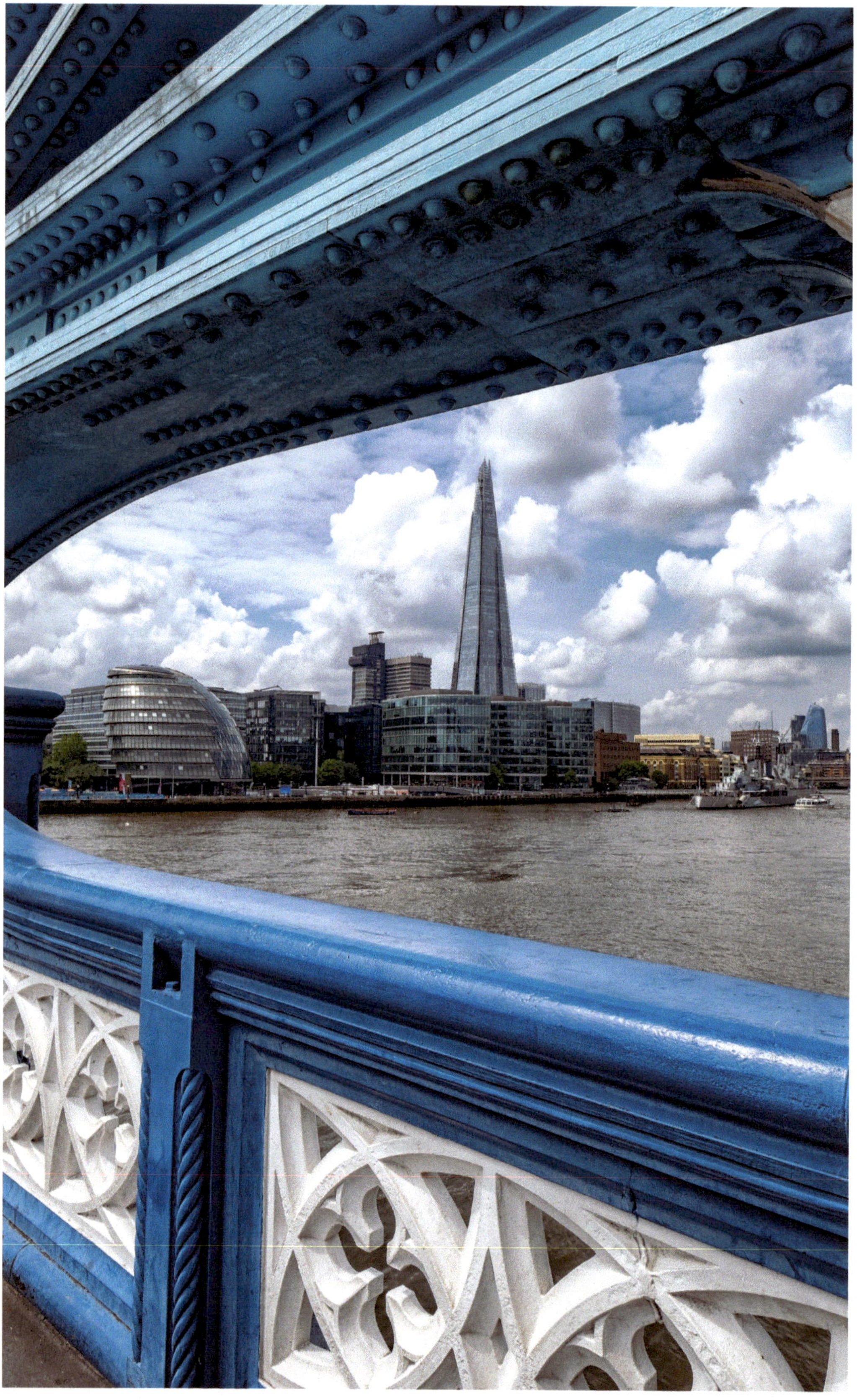